FACES OF LEARNING

50 Powerful Stories of Defining Moments in Education

Edited by Sam Chaltain

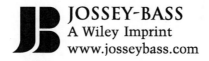

JOSSEY-BASS
A Wiley Imprint
www.josseybass.com

Published by Jossey-Bass
A Wiley Imprint
989 Market Street, San Francisco, CA 94103-1741—www.josseybass.com

Jossey-Bass books and products are available through most bookstores. To contact Jossey-Bass directly call our Customer Care Department within the U.S. at 800-956-7739, outside the U.S. at 317-572-3986, or fax 317-572-4002.

Jossey-Bass also publishes its books in a variety of electronic formats. Some content that appears in print may not be available in electronic books.

Library of Congress Cataloging-in-Publication Data

Printed in the United States of America

FIRST EDITION

HB Printing   10 9 8 7 6 5 4 3 2 1

CONTENTS

For our teachers

Inspiration, hunger: these are the qualities that drive good schools. The best we educational planners can do is to create the most likely conditions for them to flourish, and then get out of their way.

—*Ted Sizer*

INTRODUCTION

This is a book of different people's stories.

Some are about teachers who changed their students' lives. Some describe the moment when a person first discovered how to ask the right questions or found what they were most passionate about. Others are about making art or going on a challenging hike or studying everything from Morse code to *Macbeth* to kung fu. But all of the stories in this collection are about one central thing—*learning*— and what it feels like to discover one's purpose, passion, and capacity for greatness.

The fifty stories gathered here were submitted, along with hundreds of others, as part of the Rethink Learning Now campaign, a national grassroots effort to change the tenor of our national conversation about schooling by shifting it from a culture of testing—in which we overvalue basic-skills reading and math scores and under-value just about everything else—to a culture of learning, in which we restore our collective focus on the core conditions of a powerful learning environment. Our goal is to help people define what makes for powerful learning experiences, and work backward from there to decide how best to evaluate and improve our schools, our educators, and the progress of our nation's schoolchildren.

In sharing their stories, our authors—who range from students to social workers to the Secretary of Education himself—were responding to one of two simple prompts:

1. What was your most powerful personal experience in a learning community— regardless of whether that experience took place inside or outside of school?

2. Who was your most effective teacher, and what was it about that person that made him or her so effective?

The purpose in asking these questions was twofold: first, to give people an opportunity to reflect on what they already know to be true about powerful learning and teaching (rather than telling them what some "expert" thinks it is); and, second, to use the insights from these stories to help people see more clearly what a powerful learning environment actually *looks like*—and what it requires.

Based on those insights, the stories in this book are divided into five sections: Challenging, Engaging, Supportive, Relevant, and Experiential. As you read them, you'll see that most of the stories could have been listed in several categories. I also hope you'll imagine how the insights they provide can be used to strengthen the learning cultures of the schools in your neighborhood. Rather than viewing each story as a "best practice" that should be replicated and scaled up, I encourage you to think instead of how these authors' collective wisdom clarifies a "best question" we should ask whenever we want to improve our schools: How can we make schools that are more challenging, engaging, supportive, relevant, and experiential?

Now, more than ever, our country needs these sorts of schools. Unlike any other pillar of our society, public education is the only institution that reaches 90 percent of every new generation, is governed by public authority, and was founded with the explicit mission of preparing young people to be thoughtful and active participants in a democratic society. And, as these stories illuminate, the good news is that the business of improving our schools doesn't need to be a tiresome, desperate, and futile task; it can be a collaborative, risky, and deeply fulfilling journey that results in us better understanding ourselves—and each other.

In that spirit, I hope you enjoy the stories that follow. Consider putting some of the recommendations we provide at the end of each chapter into action in your life and in your community. And please take the time to share your own story, and read the stories of hundreds of other fellow citizens, at rethinklearningnow.com.

Experiential

Personal

Explorative

Relevant

High Expectations

Engaging

Challenging

Collaborative

Engaged Learner

Inspirational

Transformational

Supportive

Reflective

Caring Teacher

CHAPTER ONE

A summer art class. The United States Army. The halls of an urban elementary school. A colored high school in Apartheid-era South Africa. The streets of Philadelphia. A church basement. And three separate classrooms where it was impossible to hide.

As these stories remind us, the best learning experiences are never the easy ones. It's only when we're challenged beyond our usual limits that we have the possibility of discovering something new about ourselves, each other, and the larger world.

Meaningful learning can be risky, difficult, and sometimes painful. It can also be the moment when we first discover what we're capable of and why we can never go back to the way we were before.

JENNA FOURNEL

Hometown: Alexandria, Virginia

Job title: director of communications and outreach, Center for Inspired Teaching

Current home: Washington, D.C.

My ideal school is a place where: 'children's imaginations are revered and their individuality is honored

My personal heroes: my parents, who were my first teachers; my husband, who is a teacher; and my two-year-old son, who is my current teacher

My personal motto: No doubt the universe is unfolding as it should.

My idea of perfect happiness: watching my son discover the world; through him I am learning it all over again

My present state of mind: agitated by the slow pace of progress

My greatest achievement: raising a kind and gentle human being

Quotable: "The teacher who is indeed wise does not bid you to enter the house of his wisdom but rather leads you to the threshold of your mind."—Kahlil Gibran

---

When I was seventeen, I went to the Rhode Island School of Design for a summer precollege program. I went there to see what it would be like to be an art student and to experience life away from my family for the first time. I was a fairly sheltered child, a do-gooder who thrived on pleasing the adults in my life. As a strong student, I was unaccustomed to failure or, really, even challenge. So, understandably, many things happened that summer that would qualify as powerful learning experiences. But the one that sticks with me to this day happened in the drawing class of Bo Joseph.

Bo was an almost stereotypical artist-teacher, with his exclusively black wardrobe, passionate but sparse speech, and infuriatingly mysterious instructional style. He would give us incredibly enigmatic assignments like: "Go outside. Find something.

Make a drawing with it." And in my quest to please my instructor I would stress over the specifics of each direction, vacillating between thinking I was supposed to take them literally and searching for the higher symbolic meaning in his words. My peers did not seem so encumbered. They'd return in minutes with dog feces and popsicle sticks, creating bizarre abstract pieces that always seemed to get Bo's nodding approval. I would sit in a corner trying to draw a bird's nest with a broken twig and he would hardly give me the time of day. "That's not quite it," he would frequently say of my pieces. "I'm not seeing your inspiration yet. Keep looking."

My anxiety about his class grew and grew with each assignment as I agonized over how to create what he wanted and fell flat every time. I was baffled by the ease with which it seemed my colleagues were grasping Bo's ideas and my apparent inability to create anything that would warrant event a grunt of approval.

Finally the last day of class came, and we were to work with a live model for the first time. Bo's instructions were predictably vague: "Create." Nearly in tears, I gave up. I found my favorite corner; pulled out a large sheet of paper, a jar of gesso, and some crusty watercolor paints; looked at the model for a few moments; and started to move the paint around the paper. For the first time all summer I lost track of the students around me, lost track of time, lost track of that tall figure in black for whom I'd failed in every artistic performance. It was just me, the model, the paint, and something in my head that was telling me what to do. "Finally," said a voice out of nowhere. I awoke from my reverie to see a familiar shadow across the page. I looked up at Bo and cowered in anticipation of his critique. He lowered himself to my level and looked straight into my eyes. "You've heard your inner voice," he said. "Now don't you ever, *ever*, stop listening."

Years later, after being a teacher myself, I know that Bo took on a brave experiment with me. I like to believe he knew it would work, but I shudder to think what I would have become without the breakthrough he inspired. He saw that my desire to please was hampering my ability to create and he pushed and pushed and pushed until I got past the quest for outside approval and found my inner self. The picture is nothing outstanding. It's a reclining nude made of thick gesso with green and blue watercolor paint that has fallen into various scratches and recesses along the form. But I consider it the first piece of art I ever created.

MARK ROCKEYMOORE

Hometown: Paducah, Texas

Job title: fellow, Global Policy Solutions Inc.

Current home: Washington, D.C.

My ideal school is a place where: learning is emphasized as a lifelong process, and the skills for living a life of curiosity and exploration are fostered from the earliest ages

My personal heroes: my parents, sacrificial avatars, children from abusive backgrounds

My personal motto: life in the now

My idea of perfect happiness: perfect peace

My present state of mind: manifesting innate potential

My greatest achievement: fatherhood

Quotable: If you feel what I'm saying, it means that somewhere within you, you already know it as truth.

━ ─ ─ ─ ─ ─ ─ ─ ━

In 1987, when I was a very young man, I joined the army and went to basic training at Fort Jackson in Columbia, South Carolina, and then advanced individual training at the signal center in Augusta, Georgia. I did well on the Army Services Vocational Aptitude Battery and chose to train as a single-channel radio operator, which was a combat military occupational specialty that also gave me access to both the GI Bill and the Army College Fund. I was also chosen to learn International Morse Code (IMC), which was an additional skill identifier. That course was one month long and consisted of sitting at a desk wearing headphones and armed with a Morse code tapper of Vietnam War vintage. I proceeded to embark upon an amazing inner journey.

The training regime was relaxed. In the first week, we were responsible for tapping out and being able to interpret three groups, repeating what we heard in our headphones. Each group consisted of five dits and dashes (didadadittydadadittyda) that represented numbers and letters. The second week we were responsible for three more, and so on, until the final group of ten that we had to learn in order to pass the course and become certified in IMC.

The first week was simple enough. I was, along with everyone else, progressing normally, and we made our quota. And then, late in the second week, something happened: I progressed from three to twelve groups in the space of fifteen minutes. The sergeant, who had been teaching there for twelve years, could not—would not—believe I'd never learned Morse code before. I remember the room was dark, our desks were side by side, and the groups blended together like a song. One moment I was listening and tapping code, understanding some and having to think to get the meanings of other letters and numbers, engaging in the reminiscence and recognition pattern that typifies all rote memorization learning methods. And then at some point I entered a mode of reverie, where the dits and dashes were only audible as echoes, as my mind blurred the distinction and what had been aural became graphical—there was an actual, physical bending of mental space as if I'd flexed a previously unknown muscle and switched over to another mode where, suddenly, there appeared a depiction of Morse code in a perfect pattern of resonance and harmonics. It was as if I'd entered a hidden space that was infinite in nature.

I remember the sensation of openness, impossibly deep within my mind, and of texture and depth beyond my current needs available and waiting for input. As I was listening and experiencing this, my fingers moved faster and I instantly knew the code, could see the code, and could utilize this precious insight to cement my understanding. Coming out of it, that unknown muscle flexed once again, leaving me drained but utterly clear, excited beyond belief.

Watching the instructor walk over to me with a confused expression was confirmation that something strange had indeed just occurred. I've never returned to that space since. I've also never been challenged like that since. But knowing that it exists, having experienced it, is like a tantalizing glimpse into possibility, into the potential of the human mind to access capabilities that normally lie dormant and unused.

It is like this for us all, in every situation that leads to learning. Our ability to concentrate and utilize our innate gifts is either challenged or left unused, depending upon our desire. Whether it is in our secondary, postsecondary, community-oriented or personal educations, the choice to learn is always a choice, and our minds are often an underutilized resource, subject to distractions that engage our egocentric tendencies to the detriment of our inherent capabilities. A classroom setting can be either helpful or not, but real learning originates and comes, always, from within.

JAN RESSEGER

Hometown: Cleveland, Ohio

Job title: minister for public education and witness, United Church of Christ Justice & Witness Ministries

Quotable: "I said to my children, '...I don't ever want you to forget that there are millions of God's children who will not and cannot get a good education, and I don't want you feeling that you are better than they are. For you will never be what you ought to be until they are what they ought to be.'"—Dr. Martin Luther King Jr.

■ - - - - - - - - ■

My primary school in an upwardly mobile neighborhood of a small western town in the early 1950s was new and clean. The floor was vinyl, the walls a pale pastel. Dim round ceiling lights produced what was said to be the correct amount of light without glare. With our desks in rows, we were arranged in alphabetical order. Paragraph by paragraph, we read aloud from basic textbooks cleaned of excitement and controversy. Work completed, we were allowed to read the faded orange biographies on a shelf at the back of the room—Louisa May Alcott, Clara Barton, Daniel Boone, George Washington Carver, Henry Clay. School was one of the places I learned the virtues of compliance and obedience, what most families expected of white, middle-class American girls in that era. My classrooms represented the values of my town. Maybe this is the reason I pay a lot of attention to the physical space in the schools I visit.

At one time I assumed that school buildings that appealed to the imagination, that sparked curiosity and intellectual rigor, were settings for the education of the wealthy, but I now know that is not true.

At Chicago's Harold Washington Elementary School, hallways display collections of prints and lithographs. Along the primary wing hallway, "Harold Washington Boulevard," the late Chicago mayor's polished black Cadillac sits parked against a wall mural of a police station, fire station, and the city hall. The old building, not an up-to-date space by any means, is Principal Dr. Sandra Lewis's canvas for displaying the school's values and painting high expectations. One stairwell displays framed photographs of every one of the school's families. ""As the old staircases turn up three floors, the "dead" spaces are filled with dioramas, the most memorable a tribute to the black cowboy and filled with a real, though somewhat wrinkled, cactus and a mangy stuffed coyote. A prominent marquee hangs over the entrance of the Margaret Burroughs Performing Arts Theatre, the old-fashioned, two-story auditorium filled with the original 1915 black varnished wood seats screwed to the floor. It is painted pink with life-size panels of black performers lining the walls—Duke Ellington, Aretha Franklin, Andre Watts. Dr. Lewis announces, "Our school's band, orchestra, vocal group, and dance troupe perform here." At monthly assemblies in this same space all students posting perfect attendance enter a lottery for a new bicycle.

Even though control and order are paramount at this school—students walking to the gym or the library in straight rows, students reciting in unison a memorized creed about values, respect, and expectations—Dr. Lewis announces, "At our school we have fun." The working jukebox in the principal's office makes me believe she is right. Sometimes when I'm awake in the night or driving in traffic, my mind wanders to Harold Washington Elementary School. How would I be different if I had been lucky enough to be part of such a place? How will their time at this school shape the lives of the children there? What seems sure to me is that Dr. Lewis knows that to transform the lives of her school's children, she must fill their days with much more than basic reading and math and the drilled-down test prep that is being driven by the federal No Child Left Behind Act. At Harold Washington Elementary School, education is an act of joy.

GLORIA LADSON-BILLINGS

Hometown: Philadelphia, Pennsylvania

Job title: professor, University of Wisconsin at Madison

Current home: Madison, Wisconsin

My ideal school is a place where: learning is valued, culture is celebrated, and social justice is fostered

My personal heroes: W.E.B. DuBois, Fannie Lou Hamer, Myles Horton, Septima Clark

My personal motto: It may very well be that you have achieved royal status for such a time as this!

My idea of perfect happiness: where disagreeing with me does not mean vilifying me; where having your own opinion does not mean that mine does not exist

My present state of mind: peace in the midst of chaos

My greatest achievement: Raising strong, confident African American children

＊- - - - - - - - ＊

My most memorable learning experience came as a result of being a student in Mrs. Benn's fifth-grade classroom. Despite being in a de facto segregated school overcrowded with baby boomers, Mrs. Benn was a no-nonsense, challenging teacher who wanted students to know that they were capable of learning any- and everything because they came from a nation of people who had overcome immeasurable odds.

In Mrs. Benn's class, we learned to sing in Latin, Italian, French, and German. She took our ragtag group of poor and working-class African American students all around the city of Philadelphia to sing concerts at nursing homes, community centers, and churches. However, more significant than the singing opportunities was Mrs. Benn's focus on the history of our people.

Most of us thought she must have been making things up. How was it possible that a black man had earned a PhD from Harvard? How could it be that a black man had performed open-heart surgery? Who on earth would believe in a black explorer?

Mrs. Benn assured us that these were aspects of our history that we needed to know. They were powerful reminders of who we were called to be.

LORETTA GOODWIN

Hometown: Cape Town, South Africa

Job title: senior director, American Youth Policy Forum

Current home: Washington, D.C.

My ideal school is a place where: teaching and learning are collaborative, creative, ongoing, and engaging

My personal heroes: my parents and Nelson Mandela

My personal motto: Do your best.

My idea of perfect happiness: taking time out each year to relax and rejuvenate at a yoga retreat

My present state of mind: reflective

My greatest achievement: '...raising a son who is kind and caring, loves to learn, and takes joy in what he does

Quotable: "Our deepest fear is not that we are inadequate. Our deepest fear is that we are powerful beyond measure..."—Marianne Williamson

▪ - - - - - - - - ▪

In a Cape Town colored high school rife with the inequalities of apartheid, Mrs. Hilda Levin, my English teacher, represented a beacon of hope and encouragement. She was a white teacher venturing each day into the colored neighborhood where I lived (apartheid's success was evident in our tendency to think in terms of racial categories)—a courageous act in the volatile 1980s, when such teachers were compensated with danger pay.

Barely five feet tall, she made great demands on me and my classmates. She urged me to write creatively and often. She proposed thought-provoking topics—or no topic at all. Once she got to know my interests and abilities, she offered suggestions of books to read. She taught me the rules of English grammar and assorted writing styles—all of which stood me in good stead when, three years later, I entered an American university, and was able to edit papers for fellow students.

Mrs. Levin's support extended beyond the boundaries of the classroom. Amidst the many disruptions generated by student boycotts, she remained at school late into the day to assist us with our lessons. Other times she would load a bunch of us into her car and drive us to the University of Cape Town to get a sense of campus life. From her we clearly got the message: higher education was possible for all of us if we kept working hard. She also took us to the hospital where her husband worked as a neurosurgeon to give us a taste of career possibilities. By the time I left high school, I was ready to enter university, armed not only with the skills to read, write, and analyze, but also the conviction that I could succeed.

The oppressive political regime had worked hard to convince many of us that we were second-class citizens. Mrs. Levin's words, actions, and support provided a different lens through which to view our world, one that stressed achievement, possibility, and hope. It is that vision that continues to sustain me and inform my continued involvement in the world of education reform. And whenever I return to Cape Town and reconnect with old high school friends, within moments we are recalling something Mrs. Levin taught us or said. Her voice lives on in my head, and her actions and caring attitude remain my yardstick for what a true educator really is.

BRUCE DEITRICK PRICE

Hometown: Norfolk, Virginia

Job title: founder, Improve-Education.org

Current home: Virginia Beach, Virginia

My ideal school is a place where: happy, engaged kids learn a lot

My personal heroes: artists and inventors

My personal motto: Make it new.

My idea of perfect happiness: being creative

My present state of mind: mostly optimistic

My greatest achievement: 'writing five books and "a long poem called "Theoryland"

Quotable: The great sadness of American education is that so many of the people at the top don't care about education as transmission of knowledge. They care about education as indoctrination.

■ - - - - - - - - ■

I tell this story because I think you won't want to use it, but you should. I went to one of the country's best private schools and one of the best colleges. Then two years in the army. Classes in the army were the only ones I ever took that were actually designed to be effective. It's amazing how much you can teach, and how quickly you can teach it, if you just say, "Here's the right way to do this; follow me."

So much of modern educational theory ends up being mere sophistry, positing as it does reasons for delay, reasons for different approaches, reasons for divisions in the class.

In my experience, it's better to decide what students need to know and then tell them. Respectfully, for sure. Entertainingly, if possible.

ARNE DUNCAN

Hometown: Chicago, Illinois

Job title: secretary of education, U.S. Department of Education

Current home: Washington, D.C.

My personal heroes: my mother

My ideal school is a place where: we combine passionate, caring adults, teams of students learning together by helping each other and pushing each other, and the highest expectations for everyone

■ - - - - - - - - ■

I grew up going to my mother's after-school tutoring program in a church basement on the South Side of Chicago. It is the best learning community I've ever been a part of and the best learning experience I've ever had. That is high praise, because I have been lucky enough to attend extraordinary schools and to have great professional development and learning experiences as an adult.

My mother created a unique culture. Everyone was challenged to do their best, every single day. It was the ultimate in high expectations, both for individuals and the group as a whole. There were no shortcuts or excuses. We did lots of things in teams and groups. These collaborations created positive peer pressure where we encouraged one another. Folks who were strong in one thing were helping ones who were weak in something else. We had a sense of camaraderie. We were all in it together.

Everybody was both teaching and learning. Ten-year-olds taught five-year-olds, and fifteen-year-olds taught ten-year-olds. At every stage, you were expected to continue to learn and improve, but you also were expected to help others. The older students took great ownership for how the younger children were doing. At a very young age, children felt like leaders, role models, and teachers. It also had the benefit of helping students understand what they were learning because one of the best ways to learn something is to teach it or explain it to someone else.

Because everyone was both a teacher and a learner, we were constantly pushing each other's limits. There was no valid excuse for not working hard or for misbehaving. We had clear rewards for working hard, and there was a sense of teamwork and support across age groups. Finally, there were adults in students' lives who would stay with them for the long haul. They were there day after day, week after week, year after year, through good times and bad.

Schools should combine all of those things: passionate, caring adults; teams of students learning together by helping each other and pushing each other; students constantly both learning from others and teaching others, and having the highest expectations for everyone. If every child had the chance to have that kind of learning environment, education in this country would reach an entirely different level. It would change students' lives.

ANGELA VALENZUELA

Hometown: San Angelo, Texas

Job title: professor, University of Texas at Austin

Current home: Austin, Texas

My ideal school is a place where: children are respected and valued for their sociocultural, linguistic, and community-based identities, enabling, at minimum, fully vested bilingualism, biculturalism, and biliteracy

My personal heroes: my grandparents, who helped end Jim Crow against Mexicans in West Texas in the 1950s

My personal motto: "All things work for good for those that love the Lord and are called according to His purpose (Romans 8:28)."

My idea of perfect happiness: in the loving embrace of my ancestors before me and the generations to come after me

My present state of mind: life and career always seem to be a struggle, but I am at peace with myself, my family, my community, and my God

My greatest achievement: finding my long-lost family in Mexico only to realize that they were never lost; I was

Quotable: "I believe that the very purpose of life is to be happy.... In my own limited experience I have found that the more we care for the happiness of others, the greater is our own sense of well-being.... It is the principal source of success in life. Since we are not solely material creatures, it is a mistake to place all our hopes for happiness on external development alone. The key is to develop inner peace."—Dalai Lama

■ - - - - - - - - ■

My most life-determining learning experience happened in the eleventh grade in Mrs. Eli's class in my West Texas hometown high school. I remember the first day of the school year in her class. At first—in the brief moments before class was to start—it seemed like any other eleventh-grade class. That is, pretty normal.

Then Mrs. Eli came stomping into the classroom, angrily, did a quick visual survey, and commented that we were not the class of students she had expected. "I always teach honors!" she exclaimed, before stomping back out of the classroom while mumbling something loudly about having to leave in order to go and talk to the principal about straightening this matter out.

Perhaps we were not supposed to take her attitude toward us personally, but the chill in the air was palpable. Humiliated, we all gazed at each other through the corners of our eyes and shrunk in our chairs. I attended a large comprehensive high school, so I knew only a handful of the students in the class. It remains the most silent beginning of any class I have ever taken in my life.

Mrs. Eli's return entrance was just as startling as her exit. She walked back into the classroom huffing and puffing. With her mouth twisted in anger and frustration, she continued where she had left off fifteen minutes earlier. After stirring our deepest insecurities about whether any of us could possibly "make it" in an honors class, she loudly asserted, "Well! I am not going to teach you any differently than I teach my honors students!"

That day turned out to be a turning point in my life. I read my first novel. I wrote my first twelve-page term paper. I made my first visit to the local university library. I read and memorized extended passages of *Macbeth* and *Hamlet* and was given the opportunity to read—and fall in love with—the romantic poets, including Wordsworth, Emerson, and Thoreau.

My family, church, and community imbued me with a strong, positive sense of self. Where I was lacking, however, was in academic self-esteem. Not only did I begin to genuinely cultivate a bona fide college-going identity, but this class also empowered me to imagine that I, too, could thrive in that environment. Mrs. Eli's class liberated me from a subterranean, subaltern fear that I would never be "college material."

Despite our rough beginning, Mrs. Eli stood by her word. She treated us equitably, and she was a good teacher to boot. She was always well prepared, she encouraged discussion, and she shared her love of literature with us.

I have always wanted to thank you, Mrs. Eli, for helping a nondescript, small-framed Mexican girl in exactly the way she needed to be helped at a crucial point in her life. Gracias!

CARL GLICKMAN

Hometown: Athens, Georgia

Job title: educator and writer

My ideal school is a place where: there is a curiosity, joy, and challenge in learning across the spectrum of ages and responsibilities

My personal heroes: the unknown heroes of the Civil Rights movement

My personal motto: "They did what they could."

My idea of perfect happiness: no such thing

My present state of mind: finding one's imagination

My greatest achievement: no such thing; rather, all things in one's everyday life

◾ - - - - - - - - ◾

My public life began my junior year in high school. I had a frustrating stutter. Frustrating in that I was embarrassed to speak in public and my self-consciousness made my stutter worse. It also was frustrating in that my speech was fluid when talking to my friends outside of classrooms. But inside the classroom, when called upon to speak by the teacher, my stutter would be pronounced. I was an okay academic student, fairly popular with my classmates, and even though I didn't think my classmates would make fun of me, I became almost vocally paralyzed at the thought of having to answer a question from a teacher. I am grateful for the specialists who worked with me from childhood on how to work around my stutter by learning ways to position my tongue, using easy words with soft consonants to get started, and so on. But my frustrations remained and in my first two years in high school, I found that most teachers worked out an unspoken contract with me. I would do my work, complete all my assignments, and not misbehave and they would not put me on the spot by calling on me. This held true until I had Mr. Matheson for American history.

Mr. Matheson was a handsome, smart, young teacher that the guys admired and at least some of the gals had a crush on. His way of teaching was the discussion method and he provoked students to share their perspectives about events in U.S history. But for me, he was the one teacher I dreaded the most. Why? Because he refused to play the hidden contract game, and he frequently called on me to speak up on his class. I tried various experiments to get him not to do so, such as sitting in the furthest row, avoiding his gaze, or feebly raising my hand while everyone else was frantically waving theirs. My tactic of last resort would be to misbehave so he would send me out of the room.

None of these tactics worked. In every class, he would continue to call upon me. I kept thinking, Why doesn't he leave me alone? And then after one particularly painful response to his question when I fumbled and became red in the face, he privately asked me to stay after class for a few minutes. After the class session ended, he beckoned me to the corner and said," Carl, I want you to know that I will continue to call upon you in class. I know it isn't easy for you, but no matter how long it takes, I and your classmates will wait until you have completed your thoughts because what you have to say is worth listening to."

The effect of what he said made me realize that my speech disability need not interfere with what I have to offer and that I should no longer shirk speaking in class or other public settings. Shortly afterwards, I decided to run for junior class vice president and was required to give a five-minute talk to the entire junior class of four hundred students. This was my first talk to a large captive audience and, though I did have a stumble or two, my teachers and classmates gave me a nice ovation, and many individually congratulated me afterwards.

It would be a nice closing of this story to say that from that moment with Mr. Matheson I was cured from stuttering—but it isn't true. My stutter has been reduced over the years, but to some degree has stayed throughout my life, and it continues to rear up at unexpected times. But I did become a public speaker; teaching hundreds of college students, facilitating numerous school and business meetings, and presenting at large conferences to hundreds and at times thousands of attendees.

I wish that Mr. Matheson knew that his caring refusal to leave me alone was the confidence I needed to go public.

ANDREW MARGON

Hometown: Brooklyn, New York

Job title: Seventh-and eighth-grade special education teacher, PS/IS 184

Current home: Brooklyn, New York

My ideal school is a place where: students are invested, challenged, well fed, and safe

My personal heroes: Maurice Small, an activist and food broker in northeast Ohio

My personal motto: Be open; be present; receive love; give love; be thirsty for knowledge.

My idea of perfect happiness: when we are all free

My present state of mind: contemplative

My greatest achievement: becoming a teacher

Quotable: "Strong people don't need strong leaders."
—Ella Baker

■ - - - - - - - - ■

A great teacher's lesson can give you goose bumps and, if you're lucky, mind bumps too.

Marlene was my English teacher and choir director in high school. She was everywhere. If your jacket smelled like stale cigarette smoke, she would let you have it. In the classroom, she shined some light into your lazy, dormant, misunderstood, overactive, apathetic or whatever-other-state your adolescent mind might've been in, and actually got you up in front of the class to act out a scene from George Orwell's *1984*, guiding you to draw connections between your reality and Orwell's fiction. In choir, she led diaphragm-strengthening exercises and taught us songs in a dozen different languages, once again guiding us to draw connections.

She tended to different spaces that allowed learning, growth, and positive escape. She had high expectations and high energy. Sometimes she could be downright mean. She cared for you and took her job of helping you grow very seriously. She taught to your complexities. She had the ability to figure out what you needed and a fine-tuned ear for hearing the beauty and potential in your particular voice; if it was a roar, she showed you the merit of a whisper; if it was a whisper, she encouraged you to roar.

CHALLENGING: FIVE THINGS YOU CAN DO

1. Read How People Learn

How People Learn: Brain, Mind, Experience, and School (National Academies Press, 1999) shares the findings of a two-year study conducted by the Committee on Developments in the Science of Learning. In the book, a diverse coalition of scholars report that "the revolution in the study of the mind that has occurred in the last three or four decades has important implications for education" (p. 3). In particular, the book recommends creating a challenging environment via a set of teaching practices that "help people take control of their own learning" and encourage learners to "focus on sense-making, self-assessment, and reflection on what worked and what needs improving" (p. 12). Further echoing the ideas of this chapter, the scholars report that "learners of all ages are more motivated when they see the usefulness of what they are learning and when they can use that information to do something that has an impact on others—especially their local community" (p. 61).

2. Strengthen Your Commitment to Educational Equity

The National Equity Project (NEP) believes every child has a right to a quality education. To that end, NEP coaches people to become the powerful leaders who make good on that promise. At its Coaching for Educational Equity Institute, held twice a year in the summer for educators from across the country, NEP provides the knowledge and skills needed to build the organizational culture, learning conditions, and professional competencies needed for ensuring excellence and equity in districts, schools, classrooms, nonprofit organizations, and communities. To learn more, visit www.bayces.org.

3. Equip Your Toolbox with Q.E.D.

The Q.E.D. Foundation is a multigenerational organization of adults and youth working together to create and sustain student-centered school communities.

Q.E.D. has developed and field-tested a set of tools that schools or community organizations can use to give students challenging, meaningful choices for how and what they learn. These practices and protocols are arranged in response to the following six questions:

1. What does quality learning look like?
2. How do we design challenging, personalized learning experiences?
3. How do we assess and evaluate learning?
4. What does it mean to be college-, work-, and life-ready?
5. How do we design a learning community culture?
6. How do we measure growth and assess readiness?

To learn more and access Q.E.D's resources, visit qedfoundation.org

4. Learn How to Promote High Achievement for Students of Color

In *The Dreamkeepers* (Jossey-Bass, 2009), University of Wisconsin professor Gloria Ladson-Billings integrates scholarly research with the stories of eight successful teachers in a predominantly African American school district to illustrate that the "dream" of all teachers and parents—academic success for all children—is alive and can be emulated. Similarly, *Young, Gifted, and Black* (Beacon Press, 2004) coauthors Theresa Perry, Claude Steele, and Asa Hilliard argue that the unique social and cultural position that students of color occupy fundamentally shapes those students' experiences of school, and that a proper understanding of the forces at work can lead to practical, powerful methods for promoting high achievement at all levels. And Sonia Nieto's *The Light in Their Eyes* (Teachers College Press, 2009), now in its tenth edition, considers recent theories, policies, and practices about the variability in student learning and culturally responsive pedagogy and examines the importance of student and teacher voice in research and practice.

5. Become Skilled in Critical Friendship

The School Reform Initiative (SRI) supports the development of professional learning communities in schools: groups of educators with a common interest in improving educator practice in order to ensure challenging learning environments, high student achievement, and equitable outcomes for all students. They do this through the development of critical friendship focused on transformational learning and courageous conversations.

SRI members are committed to making their practice public to one another, being reflective, and holding each other accountable for meeting the needs and interests of all students. Through critical friendship, educators share resources and ideas, support each other in implementing new practices, and build relationships among colleagues characterized by mutual trust and freedom from judgment, while keeping a keen focus on issues of equity. They work most often in ongoing, collaborative groups, where they freely discuss each other's practice with the intention of improving student learning. To learn more about SRI and access its rich list of dialogue protocols, visit http://schoolreforminitiative.org.

Personal
Experiential
Explorative
Relevant
High Expectations
Challenging
Engaging
Collaborative
Engaged Learner
Inspirational
Transformational
Supportive
Reflective
Caring Teacher

CHAPTER TWO

Two classrooms of students on opposite sides of the globe. A search for "best questions." A roving band of Gregorian chanters. Astute observations of the obvious. Quiet time at the Acropolis. Dinosaurs. Sought-after office hours. A playground. And a classroom that became a forest, a beehive, and a place to inspire bigger dreams.

The best learning experiences don't allow us to sit passively while someone else tries to stuff information into us. What we remember, and what changes us, is when a new idea comes alive thanks to our participation and when we actively engage in the search for meaning. Otherwise, why bother?

RENEE MOORE

Hometown: Cleveland, Mississippi

Job title: English instructor, Mississippi Delta Community College

Current home: Moorhead, Mississippi

My ideal school is a place where: students are safe; leadership is shared; teachers are respected and collaborative; community is deeply involved; curriculum is rich and rigorous; assessment is performance based; creativity is encouraged; and the disabled are fully serviced

My personal heroes: Rev. Clernest Moore, Dr. Martin L. King Jr., Mary McLeod Bethune, Ida Wells

My personal motto: Use whatever gift you have for the service of others.

My idea of perfect happiness: sitting on the porch with hot tea, cool jazz, and a good book, watching my grandchildren play

My present state of mind: peaceful

My greatest achievement: helping students others had written off as hopeless achieve their academic goals

Quotable: We teachers need to take charge of our profession.

■ - - - - - - - - ■

One of the most powerful learning experiences I've had in twenty years of teaching was also one of the most serendipitous. It began in 1994, after a chance meeting that summer of a few Mississippi teachers at Bread Loaf School of English campus in Vermont and a young teacher from Soweto, South Africa. That all of us found ourselves in the same small but wonderful graduate program in rural Vermont was amazing enough. However, Bread Loaf teachers are encouraged to connect their classes during the school year. We decided we wanted our students to use literature to make the historical connections between the thirtieth anniversary of the Freedom Summer civil rights activities in Mississippi and the first democratic elections taking place that year in South Africa. Thus, the Mississippi/ South Africa Freedom Project was born.

Ultimately, the project included nine different teachers and their classrooms across Mississippi, with students ranging from grades 6 through 12, and connecting via teleconference with an all-girls' school in Soweto. We read two novels: Mildred Taylor's *Roll of Thunder, Hear My Cry*; and *Waiting for the Rain*, by Sheila Gordon. Students in all ten locations read both novels and engaged in many classroom activities appropriate for their grade level and interests. While the students corresponded with each other throughout the study about the novels and issues related to the themes, the teachers maintained a parallel discussion of teaching strategies and observations.

One of the most satisfying things about using the teleconference approach to literature study was that it provided a natural way to integrate the language arts, which all our research has long shown helps students, especially struggling students, to remember what they've learned. The students even developed (without prodding from the teachers) glossaries for each other. The Mississippians offered definitions of the Southern colloquialisms in the Taylor novel, while the Soweto students interpreted the Afrikaans and Zulu terms in the Gordon story.

Among other things, these exchanges became the best possible resource for grammar instruction. Because I only had one computer in my room at that time, students had to work together in small groups and agree on the messages that would be sent. Some of the editing went on spontaneously, but just as often I would use the content of their e-mail or text messages for small-group or whole-class lessons. Suddenly, subject-verb agreement mattered to even my most reluctant students, and just as suddenly it made sense because those were their sentences in their message that was going to be read halfway around the world.

What weeks and months of grammar drills, quizzes, and tests could not do, this student-centered, cooperative learning project accomplished almost as a by-product. For me, it was an incredibly rich experience both as a teacher and as a learner. We all came to a much richer understanding of the humanity behind what for many had been only dates, events, or labels. I became convinced of the potential of teacher collaboration, whether virtual or physical, to advance student learning and my own professional development exponentially.

AMY ESTERSOHN

Hometown: Chicago, Illinois

Job title: volunteer, Learning Unlimited
(www.learningu.org)

Current home: Chicago, Illinois

My ideal school is a place where: learning takes many forms, and students ask questions to their teacher, to each other, and to themselves

My personal heroes: teachers, friends, bloggers, designers, activists, and high school students

My idea of perfect happiness: whenever I give a particularly good lesson or presentation, I get a "teacher high" (but watch out—they're addictive)

My present state of mind: optimistic

My greatest achievement: moving tables and chairs at 5 a.m. for the benefit of thousands of high school students

Quotable: "Bad artists copy. Good artists steal."
—Pablo Picasso

I attended a public school that taught me how to love learning and how to question my surroundings. My fifth-grade art teacher would welcome us into her classroom during lunchtime for drawing and painting, and we would often discuss master works by Jackson Pollock and Vincent Van Gogh. My ninth-grade English teacher would sneak me books from the high school's supply, trusting that I'd eventually return them. My eleventh-grade math teacher would get so excited while discussing a proof that he'd start sweating in the middle of a lesson and run out of class to change his shirt. I attribute my personal and professional success to these teachers and these moments in my life. These were the people who taught me to think for myself, which is the best lesson that one can teach another.

Every student deserves love and support from teachers and administrators; every student deserves to be enriched in the classroom; every student deserves to attend a school that is safe and encourages open questioning and personal growth. The future will demand international peacemakers, scientists, doctors, political activists, educators, and innovators, and if we don't have the resources to encourage all students to ask good questions and demand good answers, our future will look even more bleak.

I do not have an answer for school reform, but I do have an idea as to how students can learn to think for themselves. I volunteer for an organization in which I help college students teach free classes to high school students, most of whom are from underserved backgrounds. Our classes are hands-on, nonevaluative, and discussion based, covering topics ranging from feminism through Disney princesses to evolutionary biology. By opening up students to topics they are interested in, we inspire them to ask questions about the world around them and delve further into inquiry. Our students not only learn a few facts that could be useful for class, but they also learn how to question that knowledge, to not only ask "what?" but "how?" and "why?" I cannot tell you what our students will be up to in five or ten years from now. But I can tell you that they will be thinking more closely about the world they will be living in.

MARITZA BRITO

Hometown: Toms River, New Jersey

Job title: world language teacher (Spanish), Brick Township Public Schools

Current home: Brick, New Jersey

My ideal school is a place where: students feel comfortable and unthreatened; they learn not only academics but also life skills; they are shaped by the guidelines given to them; they learn to be productive citizens; and, most important, where they learn that they are unique, special, important, capable, and loved

My personal heroes: my parents and my children

My personal motto: Differences make us beautiful!

My idea of perfect happiness: unity

My present state of mind: saddened by the bad name teachers have gotten in some states

My greatest achievement: my two beautiful sons: they are my purpose and my greatest gift to myself and the world

Quotable: "The education and training of children is among the most meritorious acts of humankind."—Abdu'l-Bahá

Mr. Jackson was my twelfth-grade English teacher. I was a slacker. Several of my previous teachers had confirmed that fact. Mr. Jackson never gave up on me. He never came close to an insulting comment or anything that I as a hypersensitive student could misconstrue as ill-intended. I was lazy in his class, but he gave me chances. He told me he wanted me to do well. I believed him. Not only did I believe that, I also believed that he believed his subject was something truly special. We were reading *Canterbury Tales, Macbeth*, and many other writings. Mr. Jackson didn't just have us read *Canterbury Tales*: we were in it; we became part of it. I remember creating monk costumes and parading around the school chanting Gregorian chants. He stayed overnight at the school one night to roast a whole pig. Some students and their parents joined him to keep him company. The next day everybody brought in something for the feast, and, dressed as our characters, we became a part of that story. That was amazing. He didn't have to do any of that. Then came Shakespeare. I mean are you kidding me—I was way too cool for Shakespeare. Anyway, that was going to be a lot of work figuring out what in the world that weirdo was talking about. I basically was refusing to read it.

One day he called on me, and I didn't know what the question was. So I gave a ridiculous answer and waited to be humiliated. He gently responded, "Oh no, no, no, no, no." Then he delightedly squealed in his (what we referred to as his) mad professor voice, "Oh, I see!" And with the magic of his words he turned my nonsense into sense.

Did I secretly get this Shakespeare? To this day I have a huge appreciation for Shakespeare—maybe even a love—from *Macbeth* to *Romeo and Juliet* to his sonnets. Then came the kicker—the epitome of what Mr. Jackson taught us. Alexander Pope—you already know the quote, don't you? "A little learning is a dangerous thing; drink deep, or taste not the Pierian spring: there shallow draughts intoxicate the brain, and drinking largely sobers us again."

Mr. Jackson taught us to question, and to seek answers to those questions. Many other teachers focused only on getting us to sit down and shut up. They were happy if we didn't fight in the class and let the smart kids learn. Mr. Jackson saw us all as teachable. He never gave up on us. He was caring and creative. He loved and knew his subject. Most important, he didn't teach to a bunch of kids who didn't want to learn. He made you thirst for the knowledge that he had to offer. He made you question the obscure and the obvious. I am sure Mr. Jackson is no longer teaching, but he has taught me lessons that will last for the rest of my life.

KEVIN MCCANN

Hometown: St. John's, Newfoundland

Job title: vice president, MT&L Public Relations

Current home: Halifax, Nova Scotia

My ideal school is a place where: my child learns, thrives, gains confidence, plays sports, and enjoys every day

My personal heroes: my parents,.

My personal motto: Work hard. Don't be a jackass. Take care of your family.

My idea of perfect happiness: snowed in with my wife and sons, everybody happy that the day's mandate has been subverted, listening to music, playing games, jumping on beds, imagining fantastic stories

My present state of mind: hopeful

My greatest achievement: professionally, building a career in Washington; personally, building a healthy, happy family

■ - - - - - - - - ■

An homage to the teachers I remember most:

To Mr. McCarthy, who told me once that I was "a great observer of the obvious." We debated together and as a class on whether this was a compliment or not. To this day I remember that debate, and I firmly believe it is a compliment. The obvious is paradoxically elusive—a great deal of the time.

To Mrs. Conway, who taught *Macbeth* with such vigor that I reread it now, in my thirties, every couple of years. "Lay on, MacDuff!" she would shriek, and make the most uninterested student pay attention. This, after all, was a sword fight and deserved attention, even if you had to learn.

To Mr. Neary, who had the demeanor of a lamppost but the passion of a martyr when it came to physics. I remember learning about waves and the distortion of light, sitting in the dark while each desk glowed with the tools of our experiments, learning through Neary's force of will, despite our best efforts not to.

To Mrs. Chisolm, who taught me how to play saxophone and made me understand the phrase "force of nature," and who believed I had enough talent to teach the kids in grade 5 when I was just in grade 10. You cared so much about what we did that you made us care about how we did it, and you molded us so well that disappointing you would become an unthinkable act.

To Mr. Dawe, who spent a week in 1994 on Eudora Welty's "A Worn Path," and that week changed my life. How you taught was gripping, but what you taught changed how I appreciated literature, and caused me to think again about how observing the obvious wasn't all that easy after all.

It seems so clear that the most gifted and compelling educators practice their art with passion, verve, creativity, and hard work. Yet at the same time characteristics like these are hard to nurture and cultivate in an underpaid, stressful profession. My hope for my own children is to find schools where the balance has been struck; where great teachers work and thrive because they've been given the opportunity to really practice what they do and not struggle as cogs in an impersonal student-assessment machine.

MARGARET OWENS

Hometown: Athens, Ohio

Job title: senior, Stanford University

Current home: Palo Alto, California

My ideal school is a place where: children wake up and want to go; children interact with adults on an equal footing; and children leave, ready to share what they've learned and how they've grown with their parents

My personal heroes: my parents

My personal motto: If I am not for myself, who will be for me?/ If I am for myself alone, what am I?

My idea of perfect happiness: the ability to know your flaws and still love yourself

My present state of mind: an ironic mix of agitation and happiness

My greatest achievement: finding my voice and using it to stand up for myself (it's a work in progress)

Quotable: "Books have led some to learning and others to madness."—Francesco Petrarch

＋ - - - - - - - - ＋

I had recently entered the double digits when I was lucky enough to first experience "college learning." It was spring, and I was a fifth-grader. Having spent the after-school hours making up a dance to the Spice Girls and tormenting the younger brother of my friend, I made my way home from their house at 6:00 p.m., just in time for family dinner.

Dinner was not the only thing waiting for me on the counter that evening. Next to the dishes of pasta, sauce, and broccoli was a plane ticket to Greece. It had my name on it. Right there. Passenger: Margaret Owens. My parents, always the enablers of my educational experiences, had decided I should experience the world outside of our small college town. I would be accompanying my dad, the professor, and his classics class on their semester abroad to Greece.

The baby of my family, I was thrilled to be swept into the sophisticated world of college. I watched awestruck as twenty-year-olds interacted on personal and intellectual levels with their teacher; I listened intently to discussions ranging from

Aristotle and Phidias to how drunk everyone was the night before; I even talked passionately to my dad's students about where I could maybe see myself (Cornell), and what I would like to study when I attended college.

The journey from Appalachian Athens to ancient Athens certainly opened my eyes. I walked streets that were older than I could comprehend. I ate traditional Greek meals, and my father's impatience with picky eaters forced me to try even octopus. I closed drachma coins (this was before the Euro) into the hands of a gypsy boy whose bare feet and wide eyes are still vivid in my memory, along with the sick feeling in my gut that came from realizing for the first time that not everyone sleeps under a roof at night. But more than leaving me with an appreciation for a different culture, the trip gave me an understanding of exactly what education can, and should, look like.

While my fellow fifth-grade classmates sat back at home in school desks struggling to obtain the correct remainder in their long-division problems, I hiked up to the Acropolis with my dad and his students. My dad instructed us to take the first hour to just observe and imagine being an Athenian during the height of Athenian glory. To help us do this, we were to choose a few things that grabbed our attention the most to sketch and to really put ourselves in the place of an artist called upon to honor the first democratic society. This period of personal connection to the site was followed by a formal tour led by my dad, and later at dinner we all debriefed together.

I added only humor to the discussion: I asked whether the female statues whose breasts had withered away over the centuries were Amazons, the mythological female bow hunters who cut off their breast to better accommodate their bows. But I took so much away from this discussion. For the first time, I was fully inducted into the world of great teaching and learning, and it intoxicated me. That trip taught me that real learning is one of life's most liberating and rewarding experiences.

LARRY MYATT

Hometown: Sharon, Massachusetts

Job title: senior fellow, Northeastern University Project for Leadership and Innovation

Current home: Boston, Massachusetts

My ideal school is a place where: we know each other well

■--------■

When I was in third grade, I became fascinated with dinosaurs. Woolworth's used to sell small rubber triceratops, tyrannosaurs, pterodactyls and all the rest, complete with names, sizes, and sometimes their prehistoric era on the bottom. Every time we got near the store, I would beg my Mom or Dad for one more to add to my collection. I checked out every book in our small town library. I followed every lead suggested. And soon I knew about the eras and epochs, the La Brea Tar Pits, and the early giant mammals trapped therein; I knew about excavation techniques, and I knew where and why dinosaur fossils were most likely to be found.

I presented my hobby as a "learning project" in third grade, stunning the teacher with my knowledge so sufficiently that she invited in the superintendent to watch me do it again. I went to other classrooms to present. Some kids wanted to have certain ones "fight" each other in their rubbery glory, but I would clarify and point out that the mastodon and the allosaurus lived in different time periods and probably wouldn't have fought. I can safely say that dinosaurs occupied and defined a great deal of my intellectual life in that time period. I remember it as some of the richest learning that I ever enjoyed, including the abundance of corollary learning through the reference texts, novels, and photo diaries that I tracked down as a function of dinosaur explorations.

Years later, in an entry-level survey class on paleontology in college, I was stunned and saddened that the course consisted of chart after chart, list after list of sub-epochs, of zones of fossil fern forestation, graphs of climate data, and so on. I was bored and disappointed with the way the course was packaged and with its central points. I abandoned hope of further study in that area. How the lives of such interesting creatures in such a fascinating time period could be reduced to tables and charts was beyond me.

In thinking about it years later, I realized that my experience in college had been stripped of the passion and curiosity needed to pursue real learning. I also realized that if we don't provide young people with ample opportunities for play and personal passion, for choosing and pursuing at least some of the things that bring them joy and excitement, and for building on and connecting those experiences, more and more students will be deprived of the kind of learning love affair I experienced, and will decide that school and learning offer little to and for them.

JOHN GOODLAD

Hometown: Seattle, Washington

Job title: president, Institute for Educational Inquiry

Current home: Seattle, Washington

My ideal school is a place where: children and youths want to be with their teachers

My idea of perfect happiness: is that it would be boring

My present state of mind: reflective

My greatest achievement: earning my late wife's (Evalene's) affection

Quotable: The late Ralph Tyler's view of what our schools are for: whatever education is not being taken care of by the cultural surround

----

Learning is a lifetime necessity that is increasingly subtle with the aging process. Behavioral scientist Ralph Tyler, one of my mentors, was chair of my doctoral committee at the University of Chicago. At that time, he was dean of the arts and sciences division, chair of the department of education, and university examiner. And, oh yes, he taught a course each quarter.

Tyler was much in demand to chair doctoral committees, in spite of his heavy schedule at the university and his travels elsewhere a couple of days each week. Most weeks he scheduled one hour for his students—ten minutes each for six lucky students. Getting one of his ten-minute sessions was a precious accomplishment. One entered his office as Mr. Tyler was ushering out another. (I liked very much the then-university expectation of not addressing professors with the PhD as "Doctor." I have tried to follow suit ever since whenever possible.)

Tyler appeared to have endless energy. I did not fully understand until years later the incredible learning embedded in the ten-minute seminar. Whenever I thought I needed his advice, I spent considerable hours carefully deciding what to tell, ask, and discuss. As my predecessor departed into the hallway, Tyler was shaking my hand, smiling, and asking me how my wife and I were doing. Then we sat down and I began talking, as he intently listened and occasionally asked me a question—rarely speaking anything else. Then I found myself walking to the door with him, exchanging pleasantries, and heading, relaxed, down the hall, now knowing precisely how I would get around the problem in my dissertation that had brought me to his office. What learning experiences these short visits were, and Tyler only asked questions.

Which one of us solved the problem each time? Did he? I never had ten-minute seminars with my doctoral students, but I always took pains to find out whether they had done their homework before making an appointment.

SITEMBISO NCUBE MADUMA

Hometown: San Bernardino, California

Job title: special education teacher, Shandin Hills Middle School

Current home: San Bernardino, California

My ideal school is a place where: dynamic teachers empower students to explore their capabilities in various disciplines; students miss being at school when they are absent; students become functional in our society socioeconomically and politically; students are equipped to make informed decisions void of emotional persuasions and peer pressures

My personal heroes: Nelson Mandela

My personal motto: If at first you don't succeed, try, try, try again.

My idea of perfect happiness: when one is able to be instrumental in someone else's success and happiness

My present state of mind: curious about many variables of student achievement and what students think about our education system

My greatest achievement: seeing my students realize success in different ways; seeing them realize their potential and put it to use

Quotable: "Our deepest fear is not that we are inadequate. Our deepest fear is that we are powerful beyond measure. It is our light, not our darkness that most frightens us. We ask ourselves, who am I to be brilliant, gorgeous, talented, and fabulous? Actually, who are you *not* to be?"—Marianne Williamson

■ - - - - - - - - ■

I felt safe and comfortable around her. I was eager to go to school every day because I just couldn't wait to be in my English language teacher's classroom. It was not just the classroom that was inspirational—I don't have words powerful enough to describe her lessons, which took us one rung higher each day.

Mrs. Kashora's classroom was not only a learning beehive; it was also a beautiful gallery that took you to all parts of the world where you learned about a people you never met. It was a visual thesaurus, a learning tool for her students that were 95 percent English language learners. This was during a time when technological resources were limited, but this resourceful teacher used the walls of her classroom as a resource for her students. I will ever be grateful to Mrs. Kashora for instilling a sense of self-worth in not only me but in all those who were fortunate to be her students. She encouraged us and respected every effort we made to learn. From her I learned that failure is just a learning opportunity—an experience from which you come out a better person with a new approach to problem solving. From her I learned not only to value my work but also to value and respect fellow students' efforts to learn.

Mrs. Kashora's expertise was largely in the way she demonstrated reading for comprehension. I saw her dramatize Shakespeare's *Romeo and Juliet* all by herself as she read it to us. I saw her bring *Great Expectations*, *The Color Purple*, and *Their Eyes Were Watching God* on stage. One day we found her sitting on a log, dressed like Touchstone in Shakespeare's *As You Like It*. She quietly sat there until we all took our seats in anticipation. Her stage setup was breathtaking. A forest came to life in our classroom. Then she broke the silence with Touchstone's soliloquy. She passionately went through it, then started to think aloud, analyzing the speech while we were so absorbed in what she was doing. We had never seen this kind of teaching.

Mrs. Kashora was unpredictable; she had surprises for us every day. We took up roles as different characters in the books we read and demonstrated our comprehension of their roles through either art or empathy. We worked in groups or in pairs most of the time, and there was a lot of academic noise. Sometimes we had students from our neighboring school come and learn with us, and our teachers did a wonderful job of coteaching us. Mrs. Kashora's famous directive to focus our discussions on tasks at hand was, "Let me hear some academic noise, boys and girls, let me hear just that, please." Our assessments came in different forms to cater to our different learning styles. There are many great teachers in the world, and Mrs. Kashora is one of them.

ELIJAH CUMMINGS

Hometown: Baltimore, Maryland

Job title: member of Congress, United States House of Representatives

Current home: Baltimore, Maryland

My ideal school is a place where: children are encouraged to love learning

My personal heroes: my parents (Robert and Ruth Cummings)

My personal motto: We have only one life to live. This is no dress rehearsal: this is that life.

My idea of perfect happiness: the love of my family

My present state of mind: engaged

My greatest achievement: doing my best to be a good father

Quotable: What we take from others in this life will be lost when we are gone—while the gifts that we pass on to others will remain . . . and can change our world.

━ ━ ━ ━ ━ ━ ━ ━ ━

I often return to the site of my childhood elementary school in South Baltimore. As I sit there next to railroad tracks and an elevated expressway, I thank God for the leaders during the 1950s and 1960s who showed their faith in us and invested in our future.

For the children of our neighborhood, our teachers and parents were our Moses, leading us through a wilderness of prejudice and teaching us how to forge better lives.

Five decades later, shining in a corner of my mind, I still can see the inspiring words that once were etched upon our elementary school sign: "We now are becoming what we are to be," it proclaimed—a simple motto that became the road map for our lives.

As Americans, we have a compelling interest in the struggle for our future now being waged in our nation's public schools. That is why I always find the time to meet with our community's young people, their teachers, and their families.

I welcome these conversations about the importance of our public schools and our critical role as adults in forging the future of our community. I share with other parents how my father never once missed a PTA meeting—despite the long and hard hours that he worked supporting our family.

The unwavering faith and dedication that our South Baltimore community invested in my learning were the most important forces in my early life. They created a vision of hope and opportunity that, as a society, we dismiss at our peril today. We must never forget that there is no professional calling more important than the sense of vocation that motivates those who teach our children—not President Obama's and certainly not my own.

Our teachers deserve all of the support that our society can provide. We are now becoming what we are to be.

JILL VIALET

Hometown: Oakland, California

Job title: president and founder, Playworks

Current home: Oakland, California

My ideal school is a place where: play and learning go hand in hand

My personal heroes: John Dewey and Martina Navratilova

My personal motto: Play hard, have fun, respect the game.

My idea of perfect happiness: a long run; time to hang out with my family; a chance to read, write, and think; and a great meal with live music playing in the background

My present state of mind: guardedly optimistic

My greatest achievement: my family

Quotable: "Education is a social process. Education is growth. Education is not a preparation for life; education is life itself."—John Dewey

■ - - - - - - - - ■

My organization started going national about six years ago, and our first expansion city was Baltimore. On our first exploratory visit, we brought along one of our coaches, Lamarr. In his late twenties at the time, Lamarr is a big African American guy—about 6′3″ and 240 pounds. He has a commanding presence, and kids adore him.

Lamarr and I went out to visit a Baltimore elementary school to see if there might be interest in running our program. I asked Lamarr if he wanted to describe the program, since he had actually been out in the school doing it for the past couple of years. Lamarr declined, saying he just wanted to listen to me pitch and insisting that he would remain silent.

The principal came out and escorted us into his office—a typical principal's office, with the big desk and big chair on one side and the little chairs on the other side. Lamarr looked silly—this big guy in this little chair—but he sat right down, a determined look of silence on his face. I launched into the description of what we do, describing how we have one person at every school full-time who is out for all the recesses and works with the classroom teachers to teach games through classroom game time. I explained our junior coach model, where kids assume ever more responsibility for the quality of play on the school yard. And I explained the costs. The principal listened intently throughout, nodding and looking interested.

When I finished, he shook his head and said that he thought it sounded like a great program, but that it would never work at his school. I asked if it was because of the cost, but he explained it was because they didn't have recess at his school. At this point, Lamarr, who had indeed been absolutely silent up to this point, leaned forward. "But what about when the kids finish lunch and they go outside to run around?" The principal looked a little confused, and replied: "They stay in the cafeteria. We don't have recess." This didn't compute for Lamarr, so he tried again. "But what about when the teachers take the kids out for a break?" The principal looked at me and then back at Lamarr. "We haven't had recess in five years. We tried it, but our kids just don't know how to play."

"Could I take your kids out for recess?" Lamarr asked. The principal shook his head. But Lamarr was insistent. "Just give me ten minutes today at lunch. We can wait. I can show you."

An hour later, I found myself walking into the cafeteria with Lamarr and the principal. The cafeteria at this school wasn't huge, and there were probably 140 fourth- and fifth-graders literally bouncing off the walls. There were two lunch ladies, in full lunch lady garb—one standing by either door, and both looking harried and grumpy. Lamarr strode to the middle of the cafeteria, amidst this insane din, and clapped rhythmically. Nothing happened, although a few kids looked at him. The lunch ladies were staring and looking mildly concerned. Lamarr did it again and this time a couple of kids repeated the rhythm. He did it a third time, and, like magic, all the kids responded in kind. There was complete quiet in the cafeteria.

In a big booming voice, Lamarr said, "Hi. My name is Coach Lamarr. I'm visiting from California, and I'm here to run ten minutes of recess." Wild applause broke out. "But I need you to show your teachers and principals that you can cooperate, OK? So I've got three clear directions: Finish up your lunches. Clean up your spots. And line up by class in a quiet and organized way. I'll meet you all out on the yard."

The kids jumped into action, and four minutes later we were out on the yard. Lamarr circled the kids up and had them number off by threes, breaking them into three different groups to play three different games. Amid joyful squeals, the ten minutes flew by and Lamarr did the signaling clap once again. This time, the kids responded immediately. He asked everyone to circle up, and we went around so everyone could say one word that described their feeling about what just happened.

"Fun!" said one kid. "Awesome!" said another. One boy, in blatant violation of the one-word rule, said, "When are you coming back?" Lamarr explained that he hoped he could come visit next year, but for that to happen the kids would need to line back up by their classes and return to class in an orderly way. As the kids filed back to class, the principal came up to me and said: "OK, we need to talk." As he did, I looked up to see the two lunch ladies, running across the blacktop, stern expressions replaced by wide smiles, tackling Lamarr in a giant hug of thanks.

ENGAGING: FIVE THINGS YOU CAN DO

1. Read the Power of Their Ideas

In a hopeful blueprint for revitalizing America's public schools, acclaimed educator Deborah Meier discusses her own work as coprincipal of Central Park East, an alternative public secondary school in East Harlem. Meier also advocates for small classes that encourage independent, critical thinking by using real-world exercises. Her blueprint for reform calls for enclave schools with autonomy over teaching; parents' right to choose the schools their children will attend; and student participation in socially useful, school-directed work experiences.

2. Host a World Café Conversation

The World Café is an innovative yet simple methodology for hosting engaging conversations about questions that matter to a group of people. These conversations link and build on each other as people move between groups, cross-pollinate ideas, and discover new insights into the questions or issues that are most important in their life, work, or community. As a process, the World Café can evoke and make visible the collective intelligence of any group, thus increasing people's capacity for effective action in pursuit of common aims. To learn more, visit www.theworldcafe.com.

3. Identify the Attributes of a Learning Community

This is a group exercise that begins with each participant spending five minutes thinking and writing about the best learning community he or she has ever experienced. It may be a school, a church, or a summer camp. The location doesn't matter or the age at which the person experienced it—only that it was deeply meaningful to us, and real learning occurred.

In smaller groups, each person then shares his or her personal story, uninterrupted (four to five minutes each). The rest of the group takes notes and listens actively for key attributes that emerge. After a brief round of clarifying questions (one to three minutes), the group checks in with each other about what they heard (three to four minutes). Once everyone has a chance to tell their story, a central facilitator asks

each group to reflect on their list and come up with the three to five most important attributes. These do not need to be the attributes that show up most often in
the stories—a great attribute may have surfaced just once. Each list is then shared
with the whole group. The resulting list of attributes, grounded in meaningful personal experiences, should help your group ground its work going forward in two
key areas: first, the ways in which your shared culture is already aligned to reflect
what the community knows to be a powerful and engaging learning environment;
and second, the areas in which it must improve.

4. Understand Your Learning Profile

Research in neuroscience, cognitive psychology, and related fields has given us significant insight into *how* people learn. Learning experts now understand that there
is a variety of mental functions involved in the learning process and that we each
have our own individual combination of strengths and weaknesses among these
functions—as well ideas or topics we're drawn to—that influence what we're good
at doing, where we're most likely to struggle, and how we learn best. All Kinds of
Minds, a nonprofit organization dedicated to bringing this understanding of learning and learners to teachers and into schools, has developed an interactive activity
that helps people gain insight into their own learning profiles. To learn more, visit
www.allkindsofminds.org.

5. Learn to Conduct a Socratic Seminar

The National Paideia Center serves as a source of information, inspiration, and
training for those who are dedicated to transforming whole schools into engaging learning communities based on the Paideia philosophy. The National Paideia
Center's professional development offerings help educators cultivate active learning environments and teach students how to think. Participants learn how to use
a blend of three different types of instruction to enhance the literacy, problem-
solving, and thinking skills of all students. To learn more, visit www.paideia.org.

Personal

Experiential

Explorative

Relevant

High Expectations

Engaging

Supportive

Engaged Learner

Inspirational

Collaborative

Transformational

Challenging

Reflective

Caring Teacher

CHAPTER THREE

Mrs. Molin. Miss Jonah. Mrs. Kelbaugh.

Lisbeth Welch-Stamos. Juanita Cooke. Pat Zimmerman. Alex White.

Leanne and Linda. A family in Mexico. And dear Mr. Hatfield.

Our willingness to learn, when we find it, is inextricably linked to our willingness to change. That's why all of us need to feel supported for powerful learning to occur. And as these stories remind us, behind every great learning memory is a great teacher—either in school or in life—who makes all the difference, who sees us for who we are, and who helps us craft insightful, newly uncovered narratives about what we can become.

AL FRANKEN

Hometown: St. Louis Park, Minnesota

Job title: United States Senator

Current home: Washington, D.C.

Personal heroes: My dad, who is the reason I became involved in politics. I would watch the news with him when I was a kid, and I remember watching the civil rights movement unfold. We saw footage of protests where police would use dogs and fire hoses on the people marching. My dad turned to me and said, "That's wrong. No Jew can be for that." He'd been a card-carrying Republican his whole life, but that turned him. He was a man who held onto his principles and his sense of humor, and who taught me that family mattered more than anything.

My ideal school is a place where: teachers can assess the individual needs and strengths of their students and take the time to cultivate them

■--------■

Early on in my campaign, I received a note from my fourth-grade teacher, Mrs. Molin. She said she thought I might be the Alan Franken she'd taught way back when, and that I was always a smart kid. She wished me the best and sent me a check for $25. It was the sweetest note I'd received yet. So Mrs. Molin and I got together, and she was as wonderful as I'd remembered her and wound up being a major hit on the campaign trail. So I asked her to be in my first TV commercial, and she agreed. She was terrific, and I couldn't have had a better cheerleader.

But the best thing to come of it was completely unexpected. Mrs. Molin's old students started using our campaign to contact her and send her letters about what an amazing teacher she'd been and how she had touched their lives. I received one that was so touching, I read it several times and have committed it almost to memory. It said:

Dear Mrs. Molin:

You were my favorite teacher. I wasn't a very good student. I had a hard time with math, and your spelling tests were hard! But you saw that I liked art, and I remember you staying after school one day to paint a window with me. You made me feel special (loved). Now, I'm a teacher too. I teach Special Ed kids. And I try every day to make them feel the way you made me feel. And I just wanted to say thank you.

Teachers like Mrs. Molin are an inspiration. I know what she did for me when I was a student, and it's obvious I'm not the only one. We need to make sure today's students are able to learn in that kind of creative, nurturing environment, so they can find their own passions and become strong, well-rounded adults. In today's crowded classrooms, with test-driven curricula, it's hard for teachers to do what Mrs. Molin did—to be able to identify how to reach a child and then spend the time doing it. I want to make sure that students today have the same opportunities that I did and that teachers today have the same opportunities as Mrs. Molin.

JENIFER FOX

Hometown: Milwaukee, Wisconsin

Job title: founder, Strong Planet

Current home: Franklin, Tennessee

My ideal school is a place where: people are excited by learning and feel they belong to a caring community

My personal heroes: Martin Luther King Jr., Viktor Frankl

My personal motto: People are successful when they build on their strengths, rather than remediating their weaknesses.

My idea of perfect happiness: meaningful work and meaningful relationships

My present state of mind: learning, growing, loving

My greatest achievement: continued resilience in the face of adversity

Quotable: "Our deepest fear is not that we are inadequate. Our deepest fear is that we are powerful beyond measure."—Marianne Williamson

■ - - - - - - - - ■

I can remember the very first moment I knew I had strengths inside me. I was in first grade. One day my teacher, Miss Jonah, tapped me on the shoulder and asked me to come to her desk to speak with her about a story I had written. She asked me if I would please read my story to the eighth-grade class and walked with me up the stairs to their classroom.

I will never forget the feeling of facing those twenty-five eighth-grade students. I read my story, stopping every now and then to hold up a page and show the little illustrations I had drawn in the margin. At the end of my story, they burst into applause, and at that very moment, a puff of strength blew through me. Despite my having received a D in penmanship in the second grade and a C– in spelling in the fourth grade, I nonetheless believed that I had a strength for communicating ideas in writing and proceeded to live as though it were so.

When I got to high school, the self-confidence I developed over eight years of grammar school took just five months to crumble into self-doubt, anxiety, and depression. As vividly as I can recall the moment when I first experienced the swell of my own strengths, I can recall the moment when I no longer cared about developing them.

In 1975, I spent day after day in my algebra class with my hand thrust in the air hoping the teacher would call on me. Naturally, I wanted to be successful at math. I remember hoping Mr. Hayes would call on me and value my contribution to class. When Mr. Hayes wrote $6x + 5x = 33$ on the board and asked us to solve for x, my hand shot into the air. "I don't understand what x means," I said. He answered my question by demonstrating how to work the problem. When he finished solving the problem on the board for all to see, he asked me, "Now do you see?" I told him I didn't. I explained that I understood what he'd done, but I still did not understand what x meant. He turned to the rest of the class and asked them as a group, "Do you understand?" They all nodded their heads in agreement, and he said, "Well, let's move on, then." I managed to flunk this class. I lost my motivation to learn, although I continued on in my education.

When I was in my freshman year of college, I ended up having a professor whose class I felt stupid in and I was ready to drop. But my professor challenged me to stay. He told me that my strength was my intuition and said it was as powerful as any he'd ever seen. Between the moment when Miss Jonah had asked me to read my story for the eighth grade and the moment when Professor Henning pointed out that I had intuition, I alternately hated school and loved learning. In the end, it was two teachers who pointed out my strengths that got me to devote my life to education. The small things teachers say to students can have powerful impact and change lives for better or worse. Every person has something unique to contribute; learning is about figuring out what that is.

MICHELLE DURANGE

Hometown: Littlestown, Pennsylvania

Job title: first- and second-grade teacher, Rolling Acres Elementary School

My ideal school is a place where: students always come first

My personal heroes: my husband and my parents

My personal motto: Start every day as a new day.

My idea of perfect happiness: Sunday dinner with my family, especially my grandchildren

My present state of mind: peaceful

My greatest achievement: Earning my master's degree in early childhood from Shippensburg University

Quotable: "A teacher affects eternity; he can never tell where his influence stops."—Henry Brooks Adams

◆ - - - - - - - - ◆

One might wonder how a person becomes a teacher after working twenty years as a hairdresser. Twenty-nine years ago I was entering high school as a freshman. Things were pretty bleak; my family did not have a lot of money. We received every free service that was offered. I have two brothers and one sister—all high school dropouts. The odds of me graduating did not look good. You might think to yourself: "Parents—where are they?" Well, both my parents are high school dropouts. They were busy working trying to pay the bills. I have often joked that by the time I came around they were tired of fighting with all of us just to get us to go to school.

During my freshman year I missed around a hundred days of school. I passed two classes: gym and typewriting. The truant officer had been to my house several times. They knew that if they fined my parents they couldn't pay, so the school decided that the best thing for me was to place me in vocational tech. My sophomore year I entered the cosmetology program. This year was a little better, but I continued to miss days of school.

I remember that year having a sub. I immediately liked her and remember telling her that if she was my teacher I would come to school. My junior year, I walked into the class and there was the sub from the year before. Mrs. Kelbaugh was hired permanently. She pulled me aside the first day. "Do you remember telling me that if I was your teacher, you would come to school?" "Of course, I remember that, but I really didn't mean it." She went on to tell me the school had a big meeting, and my name came up. They wanted to pull me from the program because of all my absences. Mrs. Kelbaugh told them no. She wanted a chance to work with me and to help me. She told me, "I fought for you to stay in this program. Here are the new rules. If you are sick, the ambulance better pull around front, and I will make sure you are inside. If you decide to die, then I want three days notice. Do you understand?" "Yes," was my answer, but I didn't really know if I could do it.

But I did do it, and Mrs. Kelbaugh made sure I did it. I did not miss one day. She really cared about me. She worked with me, and I worked for her. My senior year I told Mrs. Kelbaugh, "I am going to work real hard this year, and I am going to get all As." Well, I did work hard, and I did get all As. I look back and I know that this was the one person who truly cared about me. She cared if I went to school, she cared if I did well, she cared about what went on in my life. She is a teacher. My life has been changed because of her. She is no different than we are, but she made a difference in my life.

ZAINAB ALI

Hometown: Laguna Beach, California

Job title: communications manager, LA's BEST after-school enrichment program

Current home: Los Angeles, California

My ideal school is a place where: everyone has an equal opportunity to learn

My personal heroes: my mother, who is also a former educator and my lifelong educator

My personal motto: When it's bad, it's still not *that* bad.

My idea of perfect happiness: my life right now, with all the bumps along the way

My present state of mind: energized and inspired

My greatest achievement: being my younger brother's self-proclaimed role model

Quotable: "Yesterday is not ours to recover, but tomorrow is ours to win or lose."—Lyndon B. Johnson

∎ - - - - - - - - ∎

My young immigrant parents came to the United States from Pakistan in hopes of achieving the American Dream. The emphasis on education ran deep though my family. My grandfather recognized that education is the only way to transcend poverty. He once wrote to me, "Let your motto be hard work, planned studies, and recreation. Struggle to make a successful life and beautify it with knowledge, love, and discipline, which is the core of the human struggle." That will never leave me.

I never had a difficult time in school. I was always a good writer, a fast reader, and I always loved learning. I was placed in honors classes in high school, where I excelled. Life was easy. But in my junior year in high school, my easy life took a turn, as my parents' relationship became tumultuous and they planned to divorce. For the next couple of years, my parents hardly resembled the doting parents they had once been. Their lives were falling apart, and they seemed to have faith in my ability to cope. The lack of attention and the volatility at home sent me on a downward spiral, feeling that if no one else cared, I didn't have to either. I proceeded to rack up truancies; I answered B for every question on a test. I stopped doing my homework and showing up to track practice.

Lisbeth Welch-Stamos noticed. Mrs. Welch-Stamos taught journalism at Trabuco Hills High School, a class I'd taken a liking to a year earlier. *The Mustang Stampede* school newspaper was my hobby and sanctuary. I had creative front-page license to write articles such as "The State of Our Union" and "The Troubled Economy," and I used the class to research topics that interested me while practicing my ad-selling skills to local small businesses. I had something I felt I was responsible for and someone who counted on me. That was enough to get me to school in the morning.

I began sitting in Mrs. Welch-Stamos's class during lunch. I was left unbothered and could read and eat or chat with her. She showed interest in what I had to say and how I felt. She always made sure I knew that she saw my potential. Even though she knew I wasn't trying anymore, she didn't judge me, and our relationship was unconditional. She asked me questions about what was going on. It was that acknowledgement that really affected me. No one aside from her had asked me what had happened or questioned why suddenly there was this massive change in my behavior and achievement. I was looking for inspiration, for motivation, and for someone to believe in me and tell me that I had to overcome my personal obstacles for the sake of my future and passions.

She was that person. She made that future success more accessible and made me realize I was only getting in the way of achieving my dreams of following in my grandfather's footsteps. She put that power in my hands. And from then on, I never questioned my ability to make it.

In the work that I do now, I meet students every week who are struggling in the same way that I did, most of whom have even less opportunity. It is all the more apparent to me that they need their very own version of Mrs. Welch-Stamos, not another test, to realize their own potential.

SUSAN OLIVER

Hometown: Huntington, New York

Job title: communications consultant

Current home: Waterford, Virginia

My ideal school is a place where: students are respected and challenged, and teaching and learning are personalized and relevant

My personal heroes: my father, an elementary school teacher and principal who dedicated his life to raising a close family and helping underprivileged children succeed

My personal motto: Give.

My idea of perfect happiness: a happy, content family

My present state of mind: thankful, hopeful, emotional, and fulfilled

My greatest achievement: still to come

Quotable: "To let the spiritual, unbidden and unconscious, grow up through the common—this is my symphony."—William Henry Channing

■ - - - - - - - - ■

One day my sixth-grade teacher, Juanita Cooke, drove me home from school so she could talk to my parents. She told them I had been given a solo in chorus that day and had rehearsed in the auditorium in preparation for the upcoming school concert. Random people in the halls, secretaries in the main office, and a custodian or two wandered into the auditorium to listen as I sang a song that launched my passion for being heard. I was as surprised as anyone that I could carry a tune. Being the youngest of five in a busy household, I could hardly rise above the din, much less hear my own melody. Miss Cooke implored my parents to enroll me in a musical theater camp to help me develop my talents, which they did. My *Pennysaver* route paid for half of the tuition, which made it all the more dear.

The camp was full of creative kids with various talents—some with professional training and experience. Although many were well beyond me, being there at Miss Cooke's urging helped me feel confident and capable of uncorking talents I didn't know I had. I can say for sure I never would have had that exposure without Miss Cooke's encouragement. Although life eventually crowded out time for me to pursue music and theater, looking back now, I believe those passions defined me. I learned to balance being humble (God gave me those gifts) with accepting praise with grace. I learned to be a leader—in a solo in a concert or on stage in a play—and I learned that you cannot bring a character to life unless you hear and understand what they think and feel. Performing on stage in front of large audiences unleashed power, inspiration, and dreams for me.

Miss Cooke, you reached deep into me and brought my talents to the surface. In so doing, you helped me define my career and my aspiration to help others be heard. My wish for my own as well as all children: may you have a teacher or other critical adult in your life who helps you realize your talents and advocates for you to find what makes you whole.

GARY COHEN

Hometown: Hopkins, Minnesota

Job title: managing partner, CO2 Partners

Current home: Wayzata, Minnesota

My ideal school is a place where: self-esteem soars

My personal hero: Buckminster Fuller

My personal motto: We don't do it because it is easy; we do it because it is hard!

My idea of perfect happiness: Knowing I am loved and loving

My present state of mind: encouraged

My greatest achievement: starting my business with my business partner, Rick Diamond, with $2,000 each and growing it to 2,200 employees

Quotable: Greatness happens when you ask.

▪ – – – – – – – – ▪

Thirty-five years ago, I was struggling to pass English. Last year I became a published author. How did I find my way from failing to where I am now? Someone took the time to "see" me.

In the sixth grade, I had a third-grade reading level and a fourth-grade math level. I struggled with graphomotor skills, low active working memory, and attention issues—none of which was really diagnosed at the time. Hardly a recipe for success in the classroom, particularly when my teachers didn't really know how to engage kids like me. So I showed up each day, sat in my seat, stared at the chalkboard, and didn't learn a thing.

It's not like my teachers didn't care. Knowing I was a struggling learner, one of my teachers asked me to spell "A" during a spelling bee.

I froze.

That moment, which seemed to last forever, still haunts me, with the images of students staring at me, whispering their advice, while the teacher's question rings louder than a fire station's horn. I knew it was a simple, easy question and that the teacher was only trying to help—which made my inability to answer even worse.

Inwardly, I crumbled. It wasn't about learning anymore; it was about my value as a person. That moment for me was the start of a downward spiral into shame, hopelessness, and defeat.

Pat Zimmerman, a special education teacher, threw me a lifeline, but I let it lie in the water for a while. Sometimes when you're drowning, you're unable to see or unwilling to accept help. But Pat persisted. She saw my potential and eventually helped me to see it, too.

When I came to Pat, I was usually demoralized and beaten. But by the end of each period with her, I was no longer slumped in my chair; I felt inspired and excited about the possibilities ahead.

Pat "saw" me. She knew that I had a voice and important things to say. She buoyed my spirits and convinced me that my mind was fine—just different. It brought information in differently, sorted that information differently, filed it differently, and retrieved it differently. She helped me see the gifts I was given instead of the deficits on which others had focused. Not only did she help me craft narratives for my ideas and my coursework, she helped me craft a narrative about who I was and what I could become.

By ninth grade, I was not only doing my grade level of work, I was coaching other struggling learners at school during my choice time. A few years later, I graduated early and in the top 10 percent of my class. In college, I triple-majored and graduated magna cum laude. I went on to cofound a call-center company and helped it grow from two employees to 2,200. And last summer, McGraw-Hill published my book.

I've passed Pat's gift forward to many in my life—as a board member, as a parent, and as an executive coach. Thanks to her, I'm able to share the value of letting go of rigid categories and labels and celebrating the different way each of us learns.

At the same time, Pat's ability to understand me as a unique learner and to help me find and value my strengths demonstrates the power of an educator who understands learning diversity—something I believe can help us transform our schools. Because there are countless students struggling in classrooms right now who are dying inside, just as I was. And I'm proof that an educator who truly understands learning can help those students find a brighter future.

CHANTALE SOEKHOE

Hometown: Brooklyn, New York

Job title: legislative and advocacy program liaison, New York Civil Liberties Union

Current home: New York, New York

My ideal school is a place where: I'm an individual in a safe and supportive learning environment, not just a number

My personal heroes: everyone in my life who has been a source of strength and support

My personal motto: Life is change.

My idea of perfect happiness: being around the people who love and understand you

My present state of mind: living in the *present*

My greatest achievement: overcoming suicidal urges over the last eleven years

■ - - - - - - - - ■

In the fall of 2003, I started my junior year of high school with an eighth-grade education level and a serious case of broken-home syndrome. I was a high school dropout about to enroll in GED classes when fate stepped in and led me to Urban Academy.

"Hi, are you a new student? I'm teaching Short Shorts this semester—you should take it."

His name was Alex White, and he was teaching a literature course about short stories. I was sitting alone, going through pages of course descriptions when he sat down next to me and started telling me about his class. I was so taken by his charm that I signed up without reading the course description and quickly found myself in over my head. There was no way I could write in-class essays! I could barely get through a story, much less analyze it and then write an essay on demand. I was embarrassed and sure I would fail miserably—until I got my first essay back.

"You're doing great with your writing. And even though you don't talk or raise your hand in class I know you're participating. I see your reactions to what to other students say and I can tell that you're with us and you're always thinking."

Alex took it upon himself to work with me to make my writing even stronger. He saw a potential in me that I had never seen in myself and cultivated it. He quickly became a mentor and a friend who encouraged me to audition for the high school musical, a decision that truly changed me. Not only had Alex helped me find my writer's voice, he dug deeper and reawakened my passion for the performing arts.

How do you begin to thank someone for changing your life simply because he cared enough to look past the surface? Although I've tried, I will never be able to express to him how much he means to me and that I think of him and smirk every time I submit my writing to a magazine or go to an acting audition. From Alex, I learned to believe in my potential and run with it. And I don't intend to stop until I've run out of ground.

EMILY GASOI

Hometown: Rochester, New York

Job title: doctoral student, University of Pennsylvania, Graduate School of Education

Current home: Washington, D.C.

My ideal school is a place where: everyone looks forward to seeing one another, there are projects that everyone's excited about working on, and objects of interest and beauty are all around

My personal heroes: William Golding (for making a reader of me), my mom (for making a writer of me), and Deborah Meier (for making an educator of me)

My personal motto: Niente senza gioia ("Nothing without joy"—the Reggio Emilia school motto).

My idea of perfect happiness: As my good friend, W. B. Yeats, is known for saying, "Happiness is neither virtue nor pleasure nor this thing nor that but simply growth. We are happy when we are growing."

My present state of mind: on the verge of making myself more useful

My greatest achievements: interviewing for an assistant position at Deborah Meier's then-new school in Boston and being hired as a classroom teacher instead; condensing my doctoral thesis topic into an intelligible, three-sentence synopsis

Quotable: Clean the lint out of your pockets, shake out your shoes—it's a new day.

■---------■

Unlike most children who choose to become teachers when they grow up, I did not enjoy much of my schooling. Beginning in kindergarten, I passed from grade to grade in a blur of academic boredom and social dread. While I did eventually attend a good alternative high school that woke me from my scholastic sleepwalk, it is my church-basement nursery school with two twenty-something teachers—Leanne and Linda—that has become the standard I use to measure the quality of other learning environments.

First, the physical space would prove to be the most open and alluring I have ever been invited to call my own. There was room for the whole class to sit in a circle to sing songs, tell stories, or play duck, duck, goose. We even had tricycles we could ride up and down the center of the room. There were boxes of dress-up clothes, kitchen supplies and empty food containers, big blocks and small colored connecting logs, marble shoots, paint and easels, and, as the year progressed, artwork and projects everywhere.

Other specific moments stand out—seemingly mundane reminiscences that, through some mysterious alchemy of experience, personal wonder, and understanding, seem to have become part of my being in ways even I do not fully understand. I remember the way the long tables where we ate together were arranged in three rows; I remember the oversized jars of peanut butter and grape jelly, and a dull knife I had to wait to use until someone else was finished deciding the right amount of each spread to put on his or her bread. There are many more seemingly isolated memories like these, and I have often wondered why some fade, while others firmly take up residence. Though I could not have articulated it then, I now understand that what my teachers cultivated among their very young charges was a strong sense of community with room for individual needs and quirks. On some level, four-year-old me must have come to experience the long tables as a symbol of our community and the ability to choose how to prepare and eat our sandwiches as a sign of our independence.

Other enduring lessons were more overt. One of the most profound lessons Linda and Leanne taught us was to recognize and care for a wounded soul. I remember one of my classmates, Francine, as a snapshot: a sad-faced girl with golden pigtails and big, watery blue eyes. I didn't like Francine at first because of her prissy dresses, her sour face, and her strange silence. When I was a little older, my mother would explain that Francine lived in an abusive household. But I didn't know that then. I just trusted my teachers. I listened to what they told me. I watched what they did.

Linda and Leanne helped us include Francine in our play. They hugged her and talked to her all the time, even if she rarely responded. Somehow, we came to understand that Francine was a vulnerable member of the pack who we needed to watch out for. And I remember clearly the day our community witnessed a sea change occur for Francine.

It took place during one of our routine morning attendance roll calls. Though saying "here" or "present" when our name was called was not the most significant thing we did, the silence that followed when the teachers called Francine's name was notable. Her teary-eyed muteness was consistently drawn out and awkward, as the teachers gave her time to respond. Those predictable silences were probably the closest that Francine came to actually expressing her overwhelming sadness to us, and they were imbued with all the frustration and gloominess in the world. Leanne and Linda never seemed annoyed by Francine's silence, but they never stopped calling her name either.

And then one day, with no warning, she smiled shyly and quietly uttered "present." Our teachers gave her a big hug, and we all applauded. Francine eventually began to talk and smile more. It was a small gesture, but my classmates and I understood that something powerful had taken place. Trust had been won, an obstacle overcome—a quiet victory for our community.

CASSANDRA CARLAND

Hometown: Keene, New Hampshire

Job title: student voice consultant, Q.E.D. Foundation

My ideal school is a place where: students have the room and time to grow

My personal heroes: my parents

My personal motto: faith, hope, love

My idea of perfect happiness: living forever on a beautiful earth with my loved ones

My present state of mind: alert, dreamy and hopeful

My greatest achievement: living alone in a foreign country

■--------■

I had been in Mexico for about a week. I had moved here to do volunteer Bible education work for English-speaking people, and I was physically ill—but mostly just homesick and lonely. But I was a New Englander, and I had driven across country and I had always been "fine"—and always would be.

I was roused from bed by persistent knocking on my door. Two girls from the congregation had shown up to check on me. They took me out to the market. They taught me useful Spanish phrases, how to barter for good prices, how to pick out ripe mangoes. I went home with them. People I have met here are always looking in your eyes. I have discovered that they are much more in tune with other people's feelings and that no one here is ever ashamed of their feelings. I am never able to fake a good mood here. "How are you?" said the father, and gave me that look. And that day began an important lesson for me: that I didn't have to be tough all the time, I didn't have to be strong all the time, and I didn't have to say I was fine when I wasn't. So I started to cry. And I said I was homesick and I missed my family. And the world didn't fall down around me and nobody thought less of me and I actually felt better. And they wrapped their arms around me and said they were my family now.

I was immediately swept up in the chaos of the household. I found myself in the kitchen, where the girls were lined up to make tortillas. Mixing the lard into the flour, kneading the dough—measuring the right amount of dough for each piece by a complicated trick of pushing it through your fist and pinching off with the thumb. Folding it into a mushroom cap and then rolling the dough. The tortillas piled up and someone pulled out a tub of butter. I had my first fresh tortilla with butter. It's like the difference between eating a cheap apple pie at a convenience store and Grandma's homemade apple pie.

Almost the whole congregation showed up for lunch. Everyone yelled, laughed, pinched, tickled, screamed. The parents call the children *mama* and *papa*, and husbands and wives call each other *mijo* and *mija* (little boy and little girl). The guys began a noisy game of pool; the chicken, chipotle, rice, and beans were orchestrated around the kitchen; the dogs barked; the horses peered into the windows.

After we had all eaten, we dispersed to get ready for a party that evening. The girls picked out my clothes, did my hair, and applied my makeup. Horrified that I was planning on wearing flip-flops, they insisted I wear a pair of cherry-red high heels they had found in my size.

At the party we watched the sun set over the ocean. I watched the couples dancing *banda*, the local Mexican dance that I was always seeing and hearing about. It's like a Mexican polka with infinite variations and varieties. Your feet are staggered with your partners, you make sure you have a good grip on the other person and then you skip over the dance floor while the guy whips you around in circles. But I had never done it. Banda was a dance that you only did with people you knew well—your wife, girlfriend, sister, cousin, or long-time friend. I had figured it out, but knew it would be awhile before I was ever out there.

A brother from the congregation came up to me as I watched the crowd. His English was about as good as my Spanish. "I worried," he said. "Why?" I asked. "You look very *triste* [sad]. I see it in your eyes," he said. I attempted the "I'm fine." But he didn't understand that English phrase. And I wasn't sure I did either anymore. I finally told him about my family and missing them. He didn't really understand much. But he understood the words for father and mother and brother and the concept of me being here and them being far away.

At the end of the night I said my goodbyes to everyone. And when I went to say goodbye to him I suddenly found myself swept onto the dance floor—banda dancing. And everyone clapped and cheered and took video, and for the first time since I moved there I found myself really laughing as I was dizzily whipped around the dance floor and he kicked up his heels and sang along to the song. And at that moment I knew I would never be alone and there were all kinds of things waiting for me to be taught.

CARRIE A. ROGERS

Hometown: Yarmouth, Nova Scotia

Job title: second-grade teacher, South Tamarind Elementary

Current home: Rancho Cucamonga, California

My ideal school is a place where: all students are able to reach their academic potential

My personal heroes: My mother (Marilyn J. Rogers), who embodies the true meaning of strength, intelligence, and kindness; my father (Robert W. Rogers) for his incredible work ethic; my brother (Christopher R. Rogers) for his quiet wisdom; and my grandparents (the late George and Genevieve Amiro), for their examples of infinite love and generosity

My personal motto: Kindness, compassion, and generosity will make this world a better place.

My idea of perfect happiness: being with the ones I love on family night

My present state of mind: seeking/searching

My greatest achievement: has yet to be realized

■ - - - - - - - - ■

Dear Mr. Hatfield,

It's Jupiter Jones from the Three Investigators Club! I know! It's been almost twenty-five years; where has the time gone? I just thought you'd like to know what happened to your favorite trio. Well, Tobi became an Royal Canadian Mounted Police officer and is now living in the Northwest Territories with her husband and new baby. Lisa followed in her father's footsteps and became a lawyer just like she said she would. And as for me, I followed in your footsteps and became a teacher.

Yes, I know! I can hear you now! You *always* told me how "brilliant" I was and you would be amazed if I didn't end up being the doctor who found the cure for cancer or the lawyer who changed the world. You always said it would be "such a waste." But before you say another word, let me say this: if I can be even half the teacher you were, I will positively affect more lives than any doctor and lawyer combined ever could. Even as I sit here with tears in my eyes, lost in a haze of some of the happiest moments of my life, I know that I will *never* find words powerful enough to express how blessed I am to have been your student.

I won't even try to come up with some cliché blurb—you know that's not my style. Just know this: *you made a difference.* Academically, your teaching methods brought me to the top of the class—a place you inspired me to hold for years to come. And emotionally—well, let's just say that when that shy, skinny, eczema-covered kid walked into your class every day, she forgot about all the humiliating taunting and teasing that brought her to tears on a daily basis—and for the first time in her life experienced true joy, happiness, and laughter. You will never know how you've changed my life.

—Jupe

SUPPORTIVE: FIVE THINGS YOU CAN DO

1. Read Yardsticks

An outstanding guide for anyone working or living with children ages four through fourteen, *Yardsticks* was written for teachers and parents, and offers clear and concise descriptions of children's development. It is a comprehensive, user-friendly reference that helps translate knowledge of child development into schooling that can help all children succeed. To learn more, visit yardsticks4–14.com.

2. Track the Aspirations of Your Students

What accounts for the difference between a student who talks about goals and one who actually reaches them? What makes the difference between a student who works hard at everyday tasks and one whose hard work leads to a promising future? The difference, according to the Quaglia Institute for Student Aspirations (QISA), is in the student's aspirations—his or her ability to set goals and think about the future while being inspired in the present to reach those goals. In order to help schools and educators foster a learning culture that heightens student aspirations, QISA has developed the Aspirations Profile, which presents a visual model of the behaviors that support or hinder success. To learn more about QISA and its work helping K–12 schools put into practice (and assess) the conditions that foster student aspirations, visit www.qisa.org.

3. Invest in Student Learning *and* Development

The School Development Program (SDP), developed by child psychiatrist James P. Comer and his colleagues at the Yale Child Study Center in collaboration with the New Haven Public Schools, is a research-based, comprehensive K–12 education reform program grounded in the principles of child, adolescent, and adult development. The SDP provides the organizational, management, and communications framework for mobilizing teachers, administrators, parents, and other concerned adults to support students' personal, social, and academic development and achievement. The SDP also helps educators make better programmatic and curriculum decisions based on students' needs and on developmental principles. To learn more, visit www.schooldevelopmentprogram.org

4. Institute Morning Meetings

Morning Meeting is a powerful teaching tool for building community, increasing student investment, and improving academic and social skills. In *The Morning Meeting Book*, author Roxanne Kriete provides a comprehensive guidebook that helps K–8 teachers launch their school days in ways that support children and create the optimal environment for learning. To learn more, visit www.responsiveclassroom.org.

5. Create an Inclusive Learning Environment

Students with and without intellectual disabilities can learn powerful lessons about life, compassion, temerity, and social justice from each other. In fact, it's not always the person *without* special needs who mentors the person *with* special needs.

Special Olympics Project UNIFY is one strategy that takes the concept of inclusive sports opportunities and extends important lessons about teamwork and the contributions each of us can make from the playing field into school hallways. Introduce Unified Sports® in your school, utilize the Special Olympics inclusive service-learning curriculum Get Into It, work with young leaders on a campaign to end the use of hurtful language and name calling, and engage in a host of other activities designed to promote young leaders with and without intellectual disabilities. To learn more, visit www.project-unify.org.

Experiential

Personal

Explorative

Challenging

High Expectations

Engaging

Relevant

Collaborative

Engaged Learner

Inspirational

Transformational

Supportive

Reflective

Caring Teacher

CHAPTER FOUR

Creating a how-to computer guide. Listening to adults at the dinner table. Examining animal tracks in a creek. Helping a student teacher improve. Discovering the universality of math. Teaching a younger sister to read. Staying sober. Finding out what it means to be Indian. Watching the wheels of democracy (slowly) grind. And reading the great books—from a prison cell.

Learning is never most powerful when it occurs solely in the abstract. For real learning to remain with us, it must in some way be relevant. It must help us understand ourselves and our place in the world. And it must help us make connections we were previously unable to make.

R. DWAYNE BETTS

Hometown: Suitland, Maryland

Job title: national spokesperson, Campaign for Youth Justice

Current home: Washington, D.C.

My ideal school is a place where: learning and growth are a given and a product of a process that encourages creativity and discovery—not a series of tests and days preparing for tests

My personal heroes: James Baldwin, Etheridge Knight

My personal motto: The life you struggle for is the life you get.

My idea of perfect happiness: time with my family, time to write, and a vision for tomorrow

My present state of mind: excited about the future

My greatest achievement: marriage and fatherhood

Quotable: "First you jump off the cliff and you build your wings on the way down."—Ray Bradbury

❚ - - - - - - - - ❚

My soul looks back and wonders how I got over. How I stumbled past classrooms that couldn't hold my attention into jail cells that couldn't hold my hunger for knowledge.

I've come to realize that a thousand baby steps led me to prison, steps that aren't always definable, aren't always recognizable. But the steps that took me away from the classroom are clear. I remember my eleventh-grade advanced-placement U.S. history teacher catching me with a blunt burning between my fingers. From the window, Mr. Scott watched smoke defy the gravity I thought held me down. Even then, as a smart-mouthed eleventh-grader I'd read more books than I could number. Books ranging from Chinua Achebe to James Baldwin to Sir Arthur Conan Doyle and Walter Mosley; yet those books didn't translate into a passion for school. My teachers never knew about my reading habits and never did much to support them. I can't name more than four books I read in middle school and high school as part of a school curriculum. I never had to do summer readings and never had to walk into a classroom and actually think critically about how something Shakespeare wrote years ago echoed in the happenings of the world around me.

Prison gave me a sense of urgency. The nonsense that I'd spent hours talking about on street corners was no longer as important, and I found myself with a real need to communicate, to understand what was written in the books I'd been reading for years. It wasn't that I suddenly yearned to be intelligent. I'd been educating myself since the days of reading about "Earl the Pearl" Monroe and Walt Frazier taught me what it meant to be a point guard. The problem was the schools I'd attended never emphasized the importance of reading. There are no memories of classrooms of kids all discussing what James Baldwin meant when he wrote *Notes of a Native Son* or what was behind Ellison's *Invisible Man*. I began to pursue these questions for myself in prison; I began to pursue these questions with men around me who thought it important to fill the air with discussion on the meanings of metaphors. But more than this, in prison my view of the world expanded as I read writers from other nations and other countries.

Suddenly I could concentrate in a cell, where the noise of a hundred men intruded on every word written. Yet it's not prison that was the learning environment that paved my way to academic success. The unique learning environment I found myself in existed between the pages of countless books and the banging back and forth of voices that thought there was importance in challenging what a word written made you believe. School had long been an exercise in the rote—I made my own curriculum based on creating connections between the worlds of Ellison, Wright, Shakespeare, Hayden, and every fantasy novel, romance novel, and comic book that kept me turning the pages. I took those threads and connected them to the life around me by bringing them up in conversation, by recommending the books. I did for myself what a classroom never did. I made my education revolve around the literature of men trying to explain the world they lived in to themselves.

ROBERT MCLAUGHLIN

Hometown: Baltimore, Maryland

Job title: administrator, professional educator program approval, New Hampshire Department of Education

Current home: Concord, New Hampshire

My ideal school is a place where: students develop essential skills by participating in efforts to apply the skills to real-world challenges facing their community

My personal heroes: my children

My personal motto: Let's not design stress in, it'll find us anyway.

My idea of perfect happiness: a day with puppies and children

My present state of mind: sad, hopeful, and determined

My greatest achievement: being a loving father

Quotable: The measure of our lives is what we hold clear in our hearts.

■ - - - - - - - - - ■

In February some years ago, I was asked to teach a seventh- and eighth-grade combined classroom in a small rural K–8 school for the rest of the year. I didn't know the students. So, I realized, I needed to do all I could to get to know them as quickly as possible. Among the many things we did together, I asked some of the brawnier kids to take some computers (they were much heavier then) out of a storage closet and set them up.

This one seventh-grader—I'd read the file on his test scores the night before—was supposedly able to read only at the first-grade level. He set up one of the computers, pulled out the manual (computer manuals were not very readable back then), and then properly connected the keyboard and monitor. He then, to my amazement, looked through the manual and started to enter a program in BASIC. I asked him how he knew to do this. "Oh, it's no sweat, the manual lays it all out," he said. "Say, would you mind creating a how-to guide for the other kids, helping them learn to do what you just did?" I asked. "You bet," he said. I gave him a couple weeks to work on this.

A week later, his mom came for the parent-teacher conference. "What have you done to my boy?" she asked angrily. "What do you mean?" I gulped. "What have you done to my boy?" She insisted. "You've got him doing homework!" I then started to describe the litany of reasons why teachers ask kids to do homework, hoping one of them would make sense. She interrupted me. "Nah, you don't understand. In seven years, he's never done *any* homework. How did you get him to do homework?" For the first time, after making me sweat, she grinned. "He's spent every free moment working on this computer manual," she continued.

A week later, he brought his how-to manual to school. He gave it to me at the end of the day, so he couldn't see me assess it while he was there. I looked at it that night, carefully, knowing it was important to him. I was so happy—it was clear and very well done. First thing the next day, I gave it back to him and was eager to talk with him about it. He refused to take it back, said he'd look at it on his way home in the afternoon. The following morning, he came into class and, in front of everyone, threatened to assault me. He was quivering in anger. "You didn't even read this!" he yelled. "I put all this work into it and you didn't even read this!" He drew his fist back, ready to take me out. "What do you mean? I sure did read it," I said. "If you read it, then where are all the red marks?!" (where are all the places where mistakes are noted?). He couldn't imagine writing anything that didn't have lots of mistakes. I told him to show his manual to Ben, the "class brain," and if they could find even a single error I'd failed to note, I'd give them both $10. It was at that moment that I saw his life change: for the first time, he realized he was far brighter than he'd ever imagined. It turns out that his father was a car mechanic. He'd been helping his dad and never saw reading a complex car repair manual as requiring intelligence. So here he was, a seventh-grader, reading supposedly at just a first-grade level and fathoming a computer manual that many with graduate degrees could not understand. He unclenched his fist and gave me the biggest smile I've ever seen. I was so happy for him, seeing him realize his own undreamt abilities. But I also was worried: how many kids had I taught where I'd not lucked into tapping their abilities? What, I wondered, can we do to make sure that we awaken and affirm the abilities of all kids?

DEBORAH MEIER

Hometown: Hillsdale, New York

Job title: cofounder, Forum for Education & Democracy

My ideal school is a place where: everyone—students and adults—is having an interesting time trying to figure things out together

My idea of perfect happiness: that it isn't meant to last forever

My present state of mind: worried about the state of the country and the planet, but reminding myself that what comes next depends on us—and that includes me

■ - - - - - - - - ■

When I look back on my childhood I remember all those myriad occasions when I was in the company of people who were in the throes of trying to explain something they cared about—sometimes half to themselves and, perhaps more often, in the company of others.

The dinner table, for example. Listening in the car to the conversation of adults. Listening in to my brother and his friends. The dinner table talk was often "above my head," and I could rarely join in. Still, I listened attentively to the world I would someday be old enough to join fully—one I assumed I actually belonged to. I looked for opportunities to test out whether my ideas could contribute, and it never seemed dangerous to do so. The back and forth was sometimes like a good competitive tennis volley with an occasional overhead smash hit; other times it was a more casual attempt to try out different ways of handling the racket. Always, though, it mattered. So, too, when I was walking in the woods and discussing wild-flowers or trees with my mother—and trying unsuccessfully to absorb her knowl-edge, knowing the proper (Latin) names for them was beyond my poor memory skills (and may well explain why I didn't venture into gardening). But I accepted her dictum—that one should know the proper names. ("You wouldn't lean up against someone whose name you didn't know," she admonished as she identified each tree.)

How can our schools become such efficient settings for the young? How can our schools serve as places for walks through the woods, dinner table conversations, and long car rides to as-yet-unexplored places—places where the half-understood is an invitation, not a criticism, and ignorance is a source of excitement, not a judgment?

JAMAL FIELDS

Hometown: Santa Barbara, California

Job title: principal, Portola Elementary School

Current home: Livermore, California

My ideal school is a place where: everyone is happily engaged in meaningful learning; democracy is practiced every day, and the voices of adults and children alike ring out throughout the campus; our work and our learning are focused on making the world a better place to live; and our success is measured by the contentment and productivity of our students and staff

My personal heroes: my grandfather, who lived his life teaching kids to be good people and productive citizens, and who raised me in the same way

My personal motto: Do the right thing!

My idea of perfect happiness: spending time in the outdoors with my wife and kids

My present state of mind: enthusiastic, eager, and confident in the eventual victory of good over evil

My greatest achievement: still to come

＊- - - - - - - - -＊

"What is that?" the boy asks the old man, pointing at a spot in the mud.

"Looks like a critter track, I bet you left one, too," says the old man, looking around at the muddy footprints on the rocks near the boy.

The boy looks at his own tracks in the mud and on the rocks and asks, "Who made these?"

"That is a good question. I have a book of prints, and maybe we can figure it out."

The old man and the boy scurry up the rocks out of the creek and head to the house to get the book to see what left the track in the mud. They find the book and take it back to the creek to compare the track to those in the book and figure out that it was a skunk.

"I want to tell my mom about the skunk track!" exclaims the boy.

"Good," The old man replied, "Let's write it in our journal, so we don't forget to tell her tonight when she gets home."

They sit down and the boy tells the old man what to write and they construct a few sentences about what they saw and how they figured out what it was. They read the sentences over a couple of times in writing them, and then again when they were done, so that the boy will be able to read it later that night.

My grandfather, Frank Van Schaick, was a teacher and a principal who had retired when I was four years old so that he could help take care of me while my mom worked. This was a very special situation, and we cannot think we need to replicate the level of understanding and personal connection between a boy and his grandfather in every public school setting. But we can and should look to the conditions that made this learning experience meaningful and attempt to foster them in our schools.

I was interested in something and had some information that I wanted to expand upon. I had a knowledgeable person who was paying attention to my interests and provided new information and resources for me to use in satisfying my curiosity. Once I had learned something new, I was encouraged to pass the information on and given tools and help in doing so. The teacher was using a real-world situation to develop my strengths and help me to use my mind well in an area of interest to me. These are the attributes of effective teaching and learning. We need to support schools in which these attributes of effective teaching and learning are present and/or sought.

JENERRA WILLIAMS

Hometown: Oxford, Mississippi

Job title: second- and third-grade teacher, Mission Hill School

Current home: Boston, Massachusetts

My personal heroes: Jesus Christ, for through Him all things are possible; my parents for their guidance; my sister for her boldness; my children for their creative spirits; and all the men and women of my ancestry who not only paved the way for my success, but continue to influence it

My personal motto: Experience is the best teacher.

My idea of perfect happiness: loving and being loved without judgment, fear, or expectation

My present state of mind: a state of transition, with thoughts about change

My greatest achievement: being a good parent

Quotable: "To whom much is given, much is required."—Luke 12:48

At Mission Hill School, we publish a weekly newsletter that goes out to our extended community, both near and far. Within the newsletter is a short piece from each classroom teacher. Usually the piece is a reflection on the children's learning and growth. As I searched a few weeks ago for a topic to write, I stepped away from writing about my students' progress and instead thought I'd share a little about my own reflection as a learner.

Recently it was our student teacher Molly's last day. Every time a student teacher leaves I am filled with mixed emotions of sadness and joy. It is always sad to see someone leave who has become a part of your community. In a few short months they find their rightful places in our classrooms and in our hearts. However, I am joyful too. When student teachers leave my classroom, I feel confident that they have learned something about our school, our students, teaching, and themselves. It is in this confidence that I find my own growth. With every student teacher, I become a better mentor. I learn to ask the right questions. I learn to comfort and console and create the sometimes-necessary discomfort that makes us think harder. I learn how to hold the mirror before them that reflects the good they have done and allows them to see the challenges they have yet to conquer. In doing all this for the student teacher, I am also holding a mirror to myself. I also reflect the good I have done and acknowledge the challenges I have yet to conquer.

At the end of each semester, I too have grown a great deal. I have furthered my understanding of my teaching philosophy, my belief in what children can do, and my unyielding belief that experience in the classroom is the best teacher. I am a good teacher not so much because I had good teachers (though I did have a few), but because as a teacher I have become a good learner. I now understand how I learn best and how to learn from others. And it is when I recognize that I am learning that I become a better teacher.

PATRICK IP

Hometown: Modesto, California

Job title: student at University of Chicago, cofounder of Project Yes We Can

Current home: Chicago, Illinois

My ideal school is a place where: there is no limit to the places where students can learn; students realize everything is a learning opportunity, and to do this, they must challenge themselves every day ("Do one thing every day that scares you," as Eleanor Roosevelt proposed)

My personal heroes: my high school principal, Hugo Ramos, showed me through his own life story that obstacles in our life are not meant to stop us; they are opportunities for us to show everyone how badly we want something

My personal motto: Impossible is nothing.

My idea of perfect happiness: a local coffee shop

My present state of mind: developing my character through new experiences

Quotable: "If it's in your heart, do it."—Hugo Ramos

I had recently completed an eight-week intensive summer course at the University of Chicago when my summer math TA called to inform me that my math professor had received heavy criticism. I was startled. If you asked anyone in our class, you would have been told it was the best class they had ever taken in their life.

It wasn't that we were learning about math; we were learning about how life creates math and math creates life. It was true that he was unconventional, but that was his brilliance. He didn't mind dancing around in class to explain coordinate geometry or empathizing with the students when we did not understand the material. Instead of holding a more traditional teacher-student relationship, he made us feel like we were a team working together to understand math. He invited us into his life, meeting us at coffee shops after class. He studied with us and created an environment where when one of us succeeded, it felt like we all succeeded together. He didn't use a textbook, mostly because he believed that they were too restricting.

He didn't always stick to his lesson plans, because he would realize that tangents allowed us to create something new in the middle of class. By not using a textbook, he showed us we could learn from anywhere. And because he allowed tangents in class, he opened us to the power of ideas.

For our class final, he asked us to develop our own projects based on the math we had learned in the class. Being a Starbucks addict, my final concentrated on creating the perfect cup of coffee. It was a simple idea based on a complex algorithm that a group of Stanford engineers had actually started to work on in 2005 (resulting in the creation of the Clover Coffee Machine). I had come to the realization that everything was math—that even when someone speaks, they are placing mathematical variables together to form a set that could be later defined in a variety of surjections, injections, and bijections. I had also come to learn that learning is limitless, contagious, and everywhere.

I think we sometimes fail to realize that we are always learning and that we should never limit ourselves to one idea. It has never been great textbooks that changed our lives; it has been great teachers and great people.

GERLMA A. JOHNSON

Hometown: Detroit, Michigan

Job title: principal, Amelia Earhart Middle School

Current home: Detroit, Michigan

My ideal school is a place where: all members of the professional learning community experience positive growth in their education, with the objective of unfettered advancement of the students we serve

My personal heroes: my parents and all who step up to make something better

My personal motto: "Do what you need to do to be successful"

My present state of mind: grateful

My greatest achievement: to date, my daughters

Quotable: "The time of the lone wolf is over. Gather yourselves. Banish the word *struggle* from your attitude and vocabulary. All that we do now must be done in a sacred manner and in celebration. For we are the ones we have been waiting for."—Hopi proverb

■--------■

My learning story takes place during a serene summer on my front porch. I was seven years old. Having been empowered by the magic of reading, I decided to pass the magic on by teaching my younger sister to read. She was four. On that porch those sunny days, with patience on both my and my sister's part, we meticulously went through the lessons I had learned in school.

After going over how the letters sounded, we reviewed high-frequency words, sentences, and context clues. This took place with no basal reader, sound cards, or curriculum—just the cardboard toddler books we loved bought by our parents—usually begged piteously for in the checkout line of a market. By the end of the summer, my sister was a bona fide reader armed with this ability when she entered kindergarten. Whenever someone asked her in those halcyon days how she learned to read, she pointed at me and said, "She teached me." (Obviously, grammar came later.)

The interesting thing was that no one believed her. It was beyond their comprehension that another child just beyond the toddling stage could impart such knowledge to another. Soon it became the secret behind our smiles upon being posed that question.

The learning for me? That gentle summer taught me lessons at the age of seven that have remained with me to this day:

Knowledge is something that no one can take from you, but you are free to give.

No matter how it appears, everyone—no matter how young, old, great, or small—has the ability to teach and to learn.

Education just *is*—it is not how, who, or where.

I could make a lifelong impact in the life of another. I had to treat that realization with the honor and respect it deserved.

After navigating the switchbacks that life takes us through, I became a teacher. I remain in education to this day—both in the acquisition and the delivery of learning.

ANONYMOUS

■ - - - - - - - - ■

When I was thirty, I had the great good fortune to attend my first Alcoholics Anonymous meeting and thereby board what I think of as the great ship of AA, which was to carry me through the often stormy seas of life, one day at a time, to today, thirty-three years later.

AA is an extraordinary model of learning. There are no paid employees, and no one has higher rank than anyone else. We learn by sharing our "experience, strength, and hope" with each other. Meetings are led by volunteers who tell their stories: "what we used to be like, what happened, and what we are like now." Support—in the form of friendship, telephone calls, and getting to meetings—is offered unreservedly by members to each other. The only requirement for membership is a desire to stop drinking. Meetings are always free, and available in most areas every day of the week. The principles of the program are put above personalities, and you are advised to "take what you want and leave the rest." Learning happens at your own pace, incrementally, over time. No one lectures. The important points and the mottos are often repeated and are in signs on the walls. At any one meeting, you are likely to find someone with a PhD and someone who shines shoes—and each receives the same degree of respect, for everyone is treated as a valuable human being.

I have learned from people I thought might be most unlikely to be able to teach me anything, because when we speak with complete honesty to each other, we at once perceive how much we have in common. You hear your own story in others' stories, even when your respective paths to AA have been different, and you come to understand and learn a variety of ways of coping with life's challenges in healthy ways. I keep on learning at every meeting I attend.

AHNIWAKE ROSE

Hometown: Owasso, Oklahoma

Job title: policy analyst, National Congress of American Indians

Current home: Washington, D.C.

My ideal school is a place where: learning is fun, individualized, a place for exploring

My personal heroes: Wilma Mankiller

My personal motto: from *Pinkalicious* (my daughter's favorite book): "You get what you get and you don't get upset."

My idea of perfect happiness: lounging on the beach, with my daughter playing in the sand

My present state of mind: optimistic

My greatest achievement: my daughter

Quotable: "Let's put our minds together and see what we can build for our children."—Sitting Bull

■--------■

I am Cherokee and grew up in Oklahoma. One of the annual activities in our grade schools was to celebrate and participate in a reenactment of the Oklahoma Land Rush. We were all given covered wagons and stakes and encouraged to rush out into the playground and "stake out" our land. Some wanted the land closest to the slide, some closest to the water fountain—it all depends on your needs.

That particular year I chose land under a tree, so I could have some shade. I was excited to have what I considered the "best" land in the playground and couldn't wait to tell my dad all about it.

I don't need to go into detail on my parents' reaction to their Indian child participating in an Oklahoma land rush. What I do wish to share is that this experience prompted my father to start teaching me about my Indian heritage. We began a lifelong journey to discover what it means to be of mixed heritage and to grow up an urban Indian in America.

JAMES COMER

Hometown: East Chicago, Indiana

Job title: Maurice Falk Professor of Child Psychiatry, Yale University Child Study Center

Current home: New Haven, Connecticut

My ideal school is a place where: there is curiosity and trust

My personal heroes: Dr. Martin Luther King Jr., John Hope Franklin, Albert Solnit, Jackie Robinson

My personal motto: walk softly, don't carry a stick, but know where you are going—and know how to find and use a stick if you need it

My idea of perfect happiness: a manageable challenge that promotes self-expression and provides a fulfilling reward

My present state of mind: fluctuating hope and pessimism

My greatest achievement: a graduating senior from medical school came to see me in her first year because she was struggling to adjust; a scheduled half-hour talk turned into two hours that eventually helped her over the adjustment problem

Quotable: Relationships are to child development, behavior, and achievement what location is to real estate.

■ - - - - - - - - ■

As a high school student council leader, I was determined to eradicate all injustice—and rapidly. For me, an African American senior in 1951 in a predominantly white high school, the injustice I was most concerned about was racial prejudice. We had made progress in that I was the first head of the more-than-two-thirds white student council; we eliminated school dances when we could not integrate them; and we voted to eliminate segregated swim classes—although over the summer school officials sidestepped the problem by turning the pool into a gymnasium.

Nonetheless, they were paying attention to us.

I recall standing in the hallway one day, talking to Charles Palmer, the faculty supervisor of the council, expressing my frustration about another perceived injustice in our school and extrapolating to the issue of poverty and the denial of voting rights to blacks in the South. In an empathetic but not condescending way, he said, "The wheels of democracy grind slowly, but they grind." That comment began an understanding and a struggle to understand human and systems functioning that continues to this day.

The power of the impact was in part in the appearance, behavior, and demeanor of Mr. Palmer. He had just one arm—but I never heard an explanation or a complaint or observed a significant limitation. There was never a moment when he didn't take his student government and classroom teaching of government work seriously; on reflection it was almost as if he were coaching us for the Big Game. And perhaps most important, he was fair. I became the head of student government when he disqualified a white opponent who might well have won because he violated a key preelection rule—at a time in history when officials turned the pool into a gymnasium rather than reduce racial prejudice and promote fair play.

From that day to this, I have constantly put the concept of democracy and its impact on human civility to the test. Is it the best way? As I have observed and experienced the impact of democracy and its suppression in other parts of the world, the wisdom in his grinding wheel metaphor has grown more apparent—and the ability of a trusted teacher to incite deep and continuing thought has become more apparent as well.

The point was made sharply a few years ago, when a friend of mine challenged President Clinton on television in a gathering that was designed to show public support for a particular initiative. On the way home his driver, then a naturalized citizen, said, "You know, if you had done that in my country you would have just disappeared."

I concede, while too slow and too messy, at least the wheels grind and the struggle for a better democracy is possible.

RELEVANT: FIVE THINGS YOU CAN DO

1. Read the *Horace* Trilogy

The late Ted Sizer, one of the country's leading educators and founder of the Coalition of Essential Schools, wrote the three-volume series *Horace* to take an informed look at the state of secondary education and offer his dreams for the future.

Horace, who is a composite of the dedicated but frustrated teachers Sizer encountered in his visits to high schools across the country, still has a commitment to education, though he is being forced to make compromises at the expense of the students he teaches. To change high schools into viable learning institutions for all, the author outlines a heartfelt plea for high school reform by an educator who cares deeply about young people and making learning more relevant, engaging, and effective.

2. Experiment with Open Space Technology

In the book *Open Space Technology*, Harrison Owen provides a user's guide for those interested in using open space technology (OST)—an organic way of structuring group conversations that lets the participants decide for themselves what is most relevant for further exploration and harnesses the level of synergy and excitement found during the coffee break conversations at more traditional meetings.

As Owen explains, "OST is effective in situations where a diverse group of people must deal with complex and potentially conflicting material in innovative and productive ways. It is particularly powerful when nobody knows the answer and the ongoing participation of a number of people is required to deal with the questions. Conversely, OST will not work, and therefore should not be used, in any situation where the answer is already known, where somebody at a high level *thinks* the answer is already known, or where somebody is the sort that *must* know the answer, and therefore must always be in charge, otherwise known as control, control, control."

3. Strengthen Your Adult-Child Communications Skills

In the book *How to Talk So Kids Will Listen and Listen So Kids Will Talk*, adult-child communication experts Adele Faber and Elaine Mazlish provide a communication tool kit with a step-by-step approach to improving the relationships in *your* house. Their objective is to improve your ability as a parent to talk and problem-solve with your children. To learn more, visit www.fabermazlish.com.

4. Help Young People Make Effective Decisions

The mission of the Decision Education Foundation (DEF) is to improve the lives of young people by empowering them to make effective decisions. DEF provides training for teachers and youth counselors in creating and delivering decision skills instruction to students; a curriculum that teaches decision-making skills as a stand-alone course and within mainstream subject areas such as English, history, and advisory; resources to help educators reinforce the principles of decision quality; and partnership opportunities for schools or youth-focused organizations that want to help young people acquire, appreciate, and apply the fundamentals of good decision making. To learn more, visit www.decisioneducation.org.

5. See What Kids Can Do

What Kids Can Do (WKCD) is a national nonprofit that promotes perceptions of young people as valued resources, not problems, and advocates for learning opportunities that engage students as knowledge creators and not simply test takers. Using the Internet, print, and broadcast media, WKCD will show you how to communicate to the broadest audience possible a dual message: the power of what young people can accomplish when given the opportunities and supports they need and what they can contribute when we take their voices and ideas seriously. WKCD is a grant maker, too, collaborating with youth on multimedia, curricula, and research that expand current views of what constitutes challenging learning and achievement. To learn more, visit www.whatkidscando.org

Challenging

Personal

Explorative

Relevant

High Expectations

Engaging

Experiential

Collaborative

Engaged Learner

Inspirational

Transformational

Supportive

Reflective

Caring Teacher

A garden hoe. A deep exhalation. A child's guidance. A mother's woven words. A jagged rock face. A foam bat and padding. A dance performance. A prayer book. A golf trip—in Africa. And a good night's sleep—on a glacier.

We all learn best by doing—not impulsively or without direction, but thoughtfully, repeatedly, and with purpose. Books and classes are useful—but only to a point. We must get *out there* to discover something new—and if we are lucky and paying attention, our experiences can affect the world we inhabit as much as they affect us as individuals.

JOEL ELLIOTT

Hometown: Indianapolis, Indiana

Job title: community and youth development facilitator, Peace Corps

Current home: Tooseng village, Limpopo province, South Africa

My ideal school is a place where: individual self-awareness, social consciousness, and peace are actively pursued in equilibrium, and teachers view themselves as learners with the students

My personal heroes: Sally Kuiper, a Zimbabwean woman living in South Africa who runs provisions across the border to struggling families in her aching country; Steve "Bantu" Biko; Jackie Robinson; Bob Dylan

My personal motto: Stressin' out and bein' fake are complete wastes of time and energy.

My idea of perfect happiness: sitting under a huge tree, guitar in hand, a driving song comes forth, my beautiful neighbor children dance like maniacs on the red earth, singing and laughing and calling out my name...

Quotable: I can tell you now there's a ball 'n chain but it ain't marriage to the one you love, it's gettin' hitched to the patterns of this empty world and no longer havin' a story to tell.

■ - - - - - - - - ■

Thud. Thud. Thud. It was the sound of garden hoes being thrown into the ground, violently piercing the dry-panned ground, then being lifted up to unearth freshly loosened soil. Ed and Thokozani were digging together, but weren't making much progress. Our trainer, a friendly middle-aged American man dressed in clichéd safari garb and sturdy boots, broke in with his Massachusetts accent. "Okay, that's good, but let me show you something. Here, let the handle slide down in your hand so that gravity helps it to drive into the ground for deeper penetration." He whipped the spade into the earth. They tried again. We watched as the blades cut deep and large wedges of soil crumbled.

We were in a community garden in a rural Zululand village, and with the blazing South African sun laying bricks on our backs we took turns digging "double deep" and adding ash and compost to prepare the malnourished soil for the cultivation of vegetables that would soon provide subsistence for several families and revolutionize the community garden where we worked.

As Peace Corps volunteers in South Africa, we were participating in a three-day workshop alongside our South African counterparts, learning how to implement an all-natural and sustainable method of microfarming, which allows a family or household to grow as much food as possible in a small space without abundant water. This method is sometimes called biointensive permaculture. Our trainer was an agricultural expert contracted by Peace Corps, and our group of trainees a diverse blend of generations and backgrounds. Some of our counterparts only spoke Sotho or Zulu, so a couple of our multilingual participants translated every single statement into these languages. We learned together, patiently, in three different tongues.

Our first lesson on the circle of sustainability was held in the classroom, and until our final reflection session it would be the only lesson held indoors. The circle begins with soil health, we learned: healthy soil resists weeds and produces strong plants that naturally shade and give food back to the soil, which in turn produces strong plants. Outside, our trainer began to teach us the art of creating organic compost and involved all of us actively in the process of collecting green and brown matter and strategically stacking and mixing it in the heap. "You must actually do this now," he would remind us, "or else you won't be able to teach it later." As we dutifully constructed messy towers of soil food, we started to make new connections to the earth and to the greater purpose of our training. And then he asked us, "How does this relate to the circle of sustainability?" Several folks chimed in, describing the elements that aged compost contributes to malnourished soil and how these elements bring life to the garden, and later to human beings.

In only three days we learned how to harness nature's circle of sustainability to grow greater quantities of more nutritious food while preserving the soil and conserving resources. Throughout the process, we were not passive "learners," but active participants. We got our hands dirty and were also called upon often to reflect on how the principles of the circle were at work. Our questions spurred more dialogue and more doing. Our trainer showed more than he spoke, and when he spoke he did so clearly, concisely, and slowly, choosing only the most meaningful things to say, in part because that was his nature, but also because he knew his words would immediately be translated into two African languages. The translations gave us all a welcome space for the information to hang in the air, sink into our hearts and minds, and connect the ideas in some unexplained way to the tiny roots we placed in the now velvety soft soil in our seedbeds. The whole experience felt very real, fundamental, holistic.

When we finished the training, Zulu mothers and grandmothers from the village sang songs and danced in elegant circles, knowing that they would soon have more food and the knowledge to grow more. *Avulekile amasango, yebo kunjalo kunjalo kunjalo, iyoho amen*! The doors of heaven are open; so be it, so be it, amen! In South Africa, learning is never taken for granted, and it is not such a scandalous thing to give thanks in song to the Divine Mystery.

TERRY PICKERAL

Hometown: Washington, D.C.

Job title: president, Cascade Educational Consultants

Current home: Bellingham, Washington

My ideal school is a place where: everybody thrives; youth and adults feel connected, engaged, and safe to raise issues of concern; and leadership is expected of everyone

My personal heroes: My parents (who adopted me when I was two months old), John Glenn, Rosa Parks, and the members of the Special Olympics Project UNIFY Youth Activation Committee

My personal motto: Engage, enjoy, and pay attention.

My idea of perfect happiness: my grandchildren never experiencing war

My present state of mind: concerned

My greatest achievement: engaging youth in decision making and leadership

Quotable: We must never lose sight of the brilliance, insights, and wisdom of the young.

My best learning experiences have been the informal ones—learning from friends, family, and colleagues in environments where I was motivated to learn to serve others and increase my knowledge and skills.

Recently, our grandchildren visited for the weekend, and our four-year-old grandson consistently taught me how to dress him and his sister, which type of milk they drink, how to prepare fruit for them, and how to ensure they were safely in their car seats. It was a great experience to learn from a four-year-old and his two-year-old sister.

As I reflected on my knowledge and skill development, I wondered at what grade we choose not to learn from youth, what age we choose to disregard their insights, and when we choose not to consider them wise. Implications for public education include ensuring we commit to understanding the skill, gifts, and talents of all students and engaging them in activities to enhance their competencies. And ensuring we commit to valuing youth as critical contributors to education decisions and policies that influence school vision, practices, and anticipated impacts.

ELIZABETH ROGERS

Hometown: Lexington, Virginia

Job title: communications and public affairs director, Oral Health America

Current home: South Portland, Maine

My ideal school is a place where: we are not simply recipients of information that has been defined as important and necessary, and we are challenged to think, respond, and produce our own knowledge while it is being informed and shaped by the people and things around us

My personal heroes: my female friends and family members

My personal motto: Lead by example.

My idea of perfect happiness: a day with my family that includes a hike, a swim, a good book, friends, and fresh vegetables

My present state of mind: hopeful

My greatest achievement: growing up

Quotable: "If the landscape reveals one certainty, it is that the extravagant gesture is the very stuff of creation."—Annie Dillard

■ - - - - - - - - ■

On a thirty-day course in the Wind River Range in Wyoming with the National Outdoor Leadership School, I learned to get out of my own way, to trust my instincts, and to listen to the wind. I learned how to have a great night's sleep while camping on a glacier under a tarp, how to read the peaks and valleys all around us and match those with a map, and how to move through the wilderness and leave no trace behind. I am forever grateful for those thirty days when I carried everything I needed to survive on my back, and I know now that being outside and moving will always restore my sense of peace.

STEVE MOORE

Hometown: Blue Springs, Missouri

Job title: Humanities Instructor, Seton High School

Current home: Kansas City, Missouri

My ideal school is a place where: students are encouraged and enabled to explore

My personal heroes: everyday people

My personal motto: Choice is inevitable; reflection is optional—growth requires both.

My idea of perfect happiness: a cup of coffee, a deck chair, a rainstorm, and a blank piece of paper

My present state of mind: always sifting, always pondering, always learning something new

Quotable: Change can't just be scripted then enacted; it must be authored through collaboration and inquiry.

■ - - - - - - - - ■

My mother always taught me to share, but I think she was more concerned about sharing toys and other things, not the sharing of learning. I can't quite remember who taught me to share myself. I wouldn't say I'm from a family of teachers (there are a few), but somewhere along the way I became fond of sharing things that I had figured out with others. The delight for me came in seeing that another person could bypass some sort of suffering that I had experienced.

The greatest academic suffering of my life came during college: organic chemistry. Most people have the wherewithal to run the opposite direction from a class like o-chem, but I have always been attracted to dangerous things. Never has my brain been so punished, sleep put off for so long, or my eyes burned by so many lachrymatory fumes. I agonized for a B in this class through six-hour labs, pages of reports, and acid burns (I even melted a pair of glasses), among other things.

Before I left the wonderfully dangerous world of chemistry behind for English, I had a life-changing experience; I was asked to teach. Through some miracle (or clerical error, I'm sure) I ended up being asked to do summer research with one of my professor's teams. I was excited, terrified, and honored all at once. It was a chance to earn minimum wage every day in a summer for graduate-level cancer research; I was psyched. Also, I had to teach a freshman biochemistry lab for nursing majors.

Growing up, I had been a camp counselor, youth leader, marching band section leader, and aficionado of anything that allowed me to stay away from my dorky parents for hours or days at a time. Later, in college, I became a peer advisor in a freshman dorm; today I teach high school communication arts. But before I was asked to teach, just thinking about teaching a class of my peers made me feel like I was staring over cliff.

I've always liked climbing too. As a kid, I was a tree-scaler. In high school, I discovered indoor rock gyms. Friends in college introduced me to top-roping (tying yourself onto the top of a rock face, rappelling down, and then climbing back up). It was a tense transition, going from a safe thirty feet of indoor rock holds and plush padding to more than double that of real, skin-destroying, finger-crushing, billion-year-old quartzite. Staring over the edge, you can't even remember what a climbing pad feels like. Teaching left me feeling just as exposed in the beginning. I could tell you all about the different names for failing rock climbers (like the condition called Elvis Leg that you get when you're nervous and shaky on the wall), but all you need to know is that when you fail, it's public, and the "reel me back up!" conversation never leaves you feeling accomplished.

Facing a class, you don't get a reel-me-back-up option. On the wall, there are cracks you have to stick your hands into in order to go higher. There may be spiders or razorlike spines inside, but there aren't many ladderlike rungs on the face; you have to make your own holds. You have to take what the rock gives you, add a little chalk, a lot of guts, trust your anchor, and jump.

I don't remember the first time I walked into a classroom to teach. I think I may have been light-headed (from nerves, caffeine, or the toxic fumes I was so familiar with in the chem lab). Luckily, I was not alone; I had an anchor in the room. Dr. Gary Earl was the dean of the department, my unofficial advisor, and would become like a second father to me during my two-year stint in science. He was the advocate I didn't know I deserved. It took a separation of a few years for my hindsight to focus in, but eventually I realized what a boon to my career he was. Dr. Earl is a champion of his students in every way. He assures them the knots are tied and that falls result in pendulumlike motion and not death.

Something happened on that first day that made me come back a second time. I was introduced as a person who could help, a guide for the tough waters ahead. I had almost forgotten that just a year earlier I was charting my own path through similarly stormy seas. I remembered my own lab teachers and their steady suggestions along the way. If I had to pick a moment for the conception of my teaching career, it would have been this one.

What does it take to make a teacher? There's no simple formula, I can tell you, but it isn't so strange. Share what you know with others. Convey to them that while the wind is blowing hard and the water rising, they can reach the other side. As I work through the first weeks of what I hope will be many years, I find myself looking backward with one eye, staring into the vanishing point. The other eye is looking forward at what the future holds: an exciting challenge.

JILL DAVIDSON

Hometown: Providence, Rhode Island

Job title: interim executive director, Coalition of Essential Schools

Current home: Providence, Rhode Island

My ideal school is a place where: young people and adults that are a part of the school community find ways to use their minds well and work together for the common good

My personal heroes: anyone who has ever spoken bravely in anyone else's defense; anyone who has ever changed their mind based on evidence and evolving understanding; anyone who has ever struggled to achieve a dream

My personal motto: Talk less, listen more.

My idea of perfect happiness: with family and friends at the beach, no worries, nowhere else we need to be, nothing else we need to do, and not too much sand in the tuna fish sandwiches

My present state of mind: eagerly anticipating that day at the beach

My greatest achievement: finding ways to be happy daily and sharing that happiness with my family, friends, coworkers, and community

Quotable: "Put the right letters together and make a better day."—Prince

■--------■

At Rosh Hashanah services, I sat next to my nine-year-old son, a bundle of squirmy, unsettled reluctance. By the end of the service, hours later, while not precisely alight with religious fervor, he was mentally and physically present, participating, and perhaps even enjoying himself. I believe this happened because as a learner and participant in the experience, my son was in the driver's seat—or, more accurately, in the reader's seat. At the start of the service, I gave my prayer book to someone else and let my son know that he and I needed to share and that he was in charge of the book. Over the course of the service, he began to demonstrate ownership of "his" book, turning the pages at the correct moments and following along during the Hebrew songs and prayers, demonstrating his ability with that book to himself, to me, and to the congregation.

A powerful way to teach is to let go—to physically relinquish the book, the paper in the midst of edits, the computer keyboard, the whisk in the kitchen—and participate as a companion as someone else learns. Serving as a witness and coach to a learner's experience makes sense and becomes second nature when we remember that the learner needs to have control of the experience. When I learned to teach writing in college, much of the learning surprised me in its focus on setting and behavior. The first moment of revelation to me was not grasping when to use "who" and "whom" (though that did prove to be quite enlightening)—it was learning to keep the paper under discussion in the physical hands of the writer.

As a teacher and editor, it is second nature to take control of that paper to circle a word, make a point, demonstrate with a gesture. I learned that possession is a crucial element of feeling in control, and feeling in control allows a learner to stay open to the experience. I learned to ask, "Do you mind if I point something out?" rather than assuming that my role as writing coach gave me the automatic right to do so. This simple attention to possession of experience led to amazing results and has been a fabulous tool through many teaching and parenting situations since. Letting go may be harder when my children are actually in the driver's seat, come their sixteenth birthdays. Until then, we'll work on what it feels like to be responsible for their own learning and own experiences, and every day I will find new moments to let go and enjoy the relationships that develop as a result.

RACHEL BARNES

Hometown: Chatham, Massachusetts

Job title: humanities teacher, Chatham Middle School

Current home: Chatham, Massachusetts

My ideal school is a place where: teachers bring out the best in their students and celebrate achievement, enough funding exists to provide rich learning experiences, and the community is a true partner in education. Oh wait, that's where I work now!

My personal heroes: have all been teachers. This is why I entered the profession: I went to them so often for advice and support that when I thought about the kind of person I wanted to be, I always pictured them.

My personal motto: Learn something every day. Laugh every day. Make a mistake every day. Sometimes you can do all three simultaneously.

My idea of perfect happiness: involves family, relaxation, and ice cream

My present state of mind: New York? It's kind of busy and loud right now.

My greatest achievement: is replacing the bathroom sink all by myself!

Quotable: "They say time changes things, but you actually have to change them yourself."—Andy Warhol

■ - - - - - - - - ■

The Reverend Charlie Holmes. When I was first assigned to his senior English class, I was struck by his title and wondered how much of a role his religious training would play in his teaching. I was struggling with my own understanding of religion and its place in my life, and I was fearful of how his opinions might impose themselves upon our class expectations. In short, I didn't want to have to say I believed in a God that would do the things I had witnessed in the world. I didn't even attend a parochial school, and so his title confused me further.

I needn't have worried. Several weeks into the class, our classmate April had a sneezing fit. "God bless you," Rev. Holmes said calmly. She sneezed again. "God bless you," he restated. She sneezed a third time. "GO TO HELL!" he thundered.

We stared in silence, dumbfounded. "What? Obviously blessing her wasn't working," he explained, a sly grin spreading on his face. The tension eased. April did not sneeze again.

Reverend Holmes continued to defy expectations throughout the year. He began every class with a question for the class to puzzle out. If it seemed we were all in agreement, he would ask just one more question to leave us divided. Many classes turned rapidly into shouting matches as students argued passionately about their views of the literature assigned. As the year progressed, I came to see him more as a referee than a teacher. He launched us into discussion and kept us fighting for a deeper understanding of the text.

Then there was the day we actually fought. "Come on, we have to get to the gym, and we only have half an hour. I hope it's enough," Rev. Holmes told us over his shoulder, walking briskly out the door. We followed, wondering why the field trip to the gym was necessary and what we might not have enough time for. When we entered, the floor was littered with foam bats and padding. He instructed us to sit in a circle in the center of the floor. "The school tells me you all have to learn the history of the English language and pass a test on it. It's dull and boring, but you have to remember it. Here, take a card," he said, pulling index cards off a clip board. "Each card," he continued, "has a part that must be played. When I call your part, stand up and do as I tell you." The next half hour involved Normans and Saxons beating the tar out of each other with foam bats as the history of our language took shape through our actions and words. The blows from these weapons didn't hurt, but they certainly caught our attention and reinforced points. Bats became oars as language moved from one country to another. And the Reverend Charlie Holmes had the only English class who passed the test with all As. It was also the only time I remember Rev. Holmes telling us a lie: it was anything but boring.

The magic of Reverend Holmes' teaching was his understanding that our learning had to mean something to each of us in order to stay with us. He guided us all to the knowledge and beliefs we took away, showing us how to get there ourselves. He placed high value on inquiry and encouraged us to dig deeper with every class. Most important, he taught us that disagreement can be done in a respectful way and can help foster growth. It was safe to stand up for what you believed in and just as safe to change your mind. Class was, after all, a place for the unexpected to happen.

STEDMAN GRAHAM

Hometown: Whitesboro, New Jersey

Job title: chairman and CEO, Stedman Graham & Associates

Current home: Chicago, Illinois

My ideal school is a place where: the focus is on making sure information is relevant to who the children are—and who they want to become

My personal heroes: Nelson Mandela, Mahatma Gandhi, Muhammad Ali, Dr. Martin Luther King Jr.

My personal motto: Success is when preparation meets opportunity.

My idea of perfect happiness: you have the whole day to yourself, and the sun is shining

My present state of mind: focused

My greatest achievement: learning the American free enterprise system

Quotable: "You must become the change you seek in the world."—Mahatma Gandhi

■ - - - - - - - - ■

It is up to each of us to define ourselves, and that is a life's work.

Like so many others, I grew up unaware that there could be a *process* for becoming successful. Without any guidelines for *designing* a plan for myself, I was for a long time left without any real sense of direction.

Then I met Bob Brown, and my world changed.

Bob was a successful businessman and management consultant in North Carolina, where I also lived. I was a thirty-year-old employee of the prison system and unsure of where I was headed. We were both black men, but whereas I saw a world of limited possibilities, Bob's worldview was limitless. I knew this the moment I met him at a friend's house. He walked differently, talked differently—everything about him was larger, more confident, and more impressive. And it made me want to learn everything I could from him.

I got my chance shortly after our first meeting. "Do you play golf?" Bob asked me, knowing I was an active athlete. "Yes," I said—although I had grown up not knowing fully the challenges of golf and had only caddied as a young person. "Great," Bob replied. "Would you like to come with a group of us to the Ivory Coast?"

In the months and years that followed, Bob taught me about the rules of business. He taught me it was possible to dream big and to interact in different cultures and environments while remaining grounded to your essential sense of self. And, most important, he taught me that I too could achieve what I hoped for in my life.

We are all blessed in some way. In a very real sense, all of us have a certain *magic*—a gift, a talent, or an ability that if developed and put to its highest use can help us overcome setbacks, defeats, and difficulties. But we all need people like Bob to help us unearth those talents, develop the right set of skills, and start *trying* to make our way in the world.

Fortunately, we all come fully equipped with essential tools to help us as we endeavor to make our way successfully in this world. Each of us has a *conscience, a will*, and the power of *imagination*.

Most people want to stay within their comfort zones, where they feel safe and secure. But we all must risk losing control in order to push ourselves to the outer limits of our own unique abilities and talents.

Thanks, Bob, for showing me the way.

STEPHEN VICK

Hometown: Evanston, Illinois

Job title: director of child welfare, Association House of Chicago

Current home: Chicago, Illinois

My ideal school is a place where: learning is creative, interactive, and individualized

My personal heroes: William Shatner, Sir Patrick Stewart

My idea of perfect happiness: gardening with my wife in my backyard, Charlie Parker in the background, cold glass of white wine nearby, watching my three children laugh and play around me

My present state of mind: peaceful

My greatest achievement: attaining brief moments of true clarity

Quotable: "Service is the rent we pay for being ... it is the very purpose of life and not something we do in our spare time."—Marian Wright Edelman

■ - - - - - - - - ■

I sat quietly on the floor with my legs crossed. We listened attentively to our teacher as he stood still like a mountain, aged with experience and wisdom. My classmates and I took in every word and motion as he taught ancient methods for the most basic of human actions: respiration—inhale and exhale. If you were not in the class, you might find it odd—ten students sitting cross-legged behind glass walls that separated us from the hustle and horns of busy buses, cars, and passersby on the Northwest side of Chicago.

Key Chun Song is in his midsixties, short, and well groomed. His white collared sleeves are rolled once, showing his strong forearms. His face is calm and peaceful, with high cheekbones and a wisp of a mustache and goatee. He is short in stature, but gives no impression of weakness. He is solid like a tree trunk, roots sunk deep into the earth. He is unlike any teacher I have had. He speaks in broken English, yet I understand him clearly through his subtle metaphors. Maybe it is the many years I have listened to his voice, but I can easily pick out the words he stumbles over. It seems that traditional teachers, those I have had throughout my Western education, do a lot of excess talking, force-feeding the material.

Somehow, in the years I have studied under Grand Master Song, I have realized that less is more. Just as we must learn how to breathe as when we were infants, expanding the abdomen ... filling our entire chest ... we must relearn learning. How can one explore and learn creatively? Through action and experience, reflecting and revisiting—not being graded on false markers or others' predetermined expectations—passing or failing.

I sit quietly on the floor. Inhale. Exhale. My shoulders and back are relaxed. My head and spine are erect, as if being held up by a string. I am calm and peaceful, following the gentle words of my teacher. A smile is lightly present on my face, the same as the nine other students in the class. I am a baby, learning to breathe.

LIZ LERMAN

Hometown: Milwaukee, Wisconsin

Job title: founding artistic director, Liz Lerman Dance Exchange

Current home: Takoma Park, Maryland

My ideal school is a place where: students are given the tools, the support, the challenge to make sense of their world, their imagination, and their experience by reading, writing, making art, studying big questions, working alongside curious and passionate professionals in whatever field interests them

My personal heroes: my parents, husband and daughter, nieces and nephews, brothers and sisters—and artists making art in parts of the world where that act is life-threatening

My personal motto: Nothing is too small to notice; art is big.

My favorite journey: anytime I can be on the road with Jon and Anna

My idea of perfect happiness: a day in the studio when everything is going well, a day at home when there is no schedule, the night Obama won the election

My present state of mind: curious

My greatest achievement: to be a working mother and build a humane institution where personal and professional growth go hand in hand and where making quiet revolutions everyday is the expected

∎ - - - - - - - - ∎

During the five years I was in residence at Children's Hospital in Washington D.C., we did only one major performance. On that day they brought all the kids, families, and available staff down to the atrium, where we danced several pieces from our repertory. Except for the lack of a conventional stage, it was very much a full-fledged performance. One of the dances, called Bonsai, was a quiet piece that told the story of how the caretaking of these long-lived trees passes on to a new generation.

I noticed as we were performing this dance that a youngster in the front row had fallen asleep. I had met this child earlier in the week and had liked her, so I was sad to see her miss so much. As I was leaving the hospital, slightly dejected, one of the nurses ran after me and said in a very enthusiastic voice, "Thank you, thank you, we have been trying to get that kid to go to sleep for three days."

Up to that point I had thought one of the most important functions of art was to wake people up. Here I was confronted with information teaching me the opposite. I was grateful. I would never have learned this if I had stayed in the studio making my dances. If we are lucky and paying attention, we can discover over and over again that the intersection of art and real life affects the art form as much as it affects the community and the people involved.

MAYA SOETORO-NG

Hometown: Honolulu, Hawaii

Job title: education specialist, East West Center

Current home: Honolulu, Hawaii

My ideal school is a place where: the surrounding community is visibly involved and significantly impacted, where children stretch their minds, become powerfully competent, and laugh out loud

My personal heroes: Mahatma Gandhi, my mom

My personal motto: Be kind.

My favorite journey: the kind where internal and external terrain run into one another

My idea of perfect happiness: a snuggle session with my family in a giant hammock underneath a giant banyan and a full moon, surrounded by gardenia bushes with the promise of Indonesian food and strong coffee in the hour ahead

My present state of mind: humming

My greatest achievement: yeah, it's the kids

Quotable: The great challenge is to find home, even though you're aboard a ship that never docks.

Our mama taught us how to be simultaneously brave and pliant, and we found ourselves in this winning combination.

Mama Annie was my only teacher for much of my childhood. She home-schooled me through several formative years spent in Central Java, my father's birthplace. There I made note of the traditional preference that a woman not laugh too hard or be too assertive. There my peers were taught to wait, be patient, duck, and look down when passing adult men.

When I started high school in Hawaii at the age of fourteen, I noticed that American girls were generous, supportive, and cute and sought academic excellence in the form of pretty handwriting, decorated notebooks, and a strong work ethic. In contrast, teachers had a rapport with the boys, a loose banter that implied on some level that the boys were more amusing and were more their equals. Teachers said nothing when sexual remarks were addressed to girls in class or when girls were objectified when passing by boy-littered benches on campus, by being rated with signs held high bearing the numbers one through ten. I questioned my mother's judgment when she said that there were innumerable ways to be a woman, and it was then that she took my chin in her hand and, with woven words, good-naturedly upheld my right to be precisely the person I was meant to be.

By her account, Mom was precisely the woman she was meant to be. Working in highly patriarchal and socially conservative communities, she never seemed to feel silenced or pessimistic. Her optimism was brave.

Mama Annie also encouraged us to embrace the world entire. She had us study many global works of philosophy, religion, and literature. She took me with her across the longest stretches of ocean and along the dustiest of roads. She said that while we all may have some local place in the order of things, that we best serve social justice goals by being concerned about the lives of people both faraway and near. She taught me that when we accept gracefully the gorgeous challenge of living in more than one world, we free ourselves to search for fruitful shared spaces between all people. Together in those shared spaces, we can fight insularity while retaining pride in where and who we have been.

It seems that Mama Annie found great reward and respect by tearing down walls between her self and innumerable others in the world. Mama's lessons about being intellectually and emotionally flexible are so important for those of us struggling with our place in ever-changing nations and with our identities at a time when naming one's loyalties and priorities has grown more challenging.

Too often we still teach as though there is one truth or singular point of view. Through the language we use and the details we choose to share, absolutist and one-dimensional perspectives too frequently emerge. Mom would have counseled that such perspectives are impoverished and that we can find richness in negotiated understandings, as long as we learn how to become comfortable with ambiguity and multiplicity.

As my teacher, my mother gave me opportunities to reflect upon and discuss the tensions that were common to both the stories we read and the world around us. In helping me to explore heroism and villainy, good and evil, the beautiful and ugly, the spiritual and intellectual, Mama Annie showed me the importance of having both moral courage and deep empathy. We must be strong about choosing our paths, naming ourselves, and working towards greater justice, but we must be flexible and soft about understanding and cooperating with others.

Perhaps if more teachers felt okay about bringing in the wisdom of mothers, fewer students would take on simplistic assumptions about gender or other categories of culture. We can use history's storytelling and the lives of literature to show our students that neither the labels we use nor the norms we assign are inevitable. Our kids will know that they have choices as long as they can see far into the distance and begin to step bravely in every direction.

EXPERIENTIAL: FIVE THINGS YOU CAN DO

1. Take a Wilderness Course

Outward Bound is a nonprofit educational organization that serves people of all ages and backgrounds through active learning expeditions that inspire character development, self-discovery, and service both in and out of the classroom. Outward Bound delivers programs using unfamiliar settings as a way for participants across the country to experience adventure and challenge in a way that helps students realize they can do more than they thought possible. Customized courses provide curricula developed for struggling teens; groups with specific health, social, or educational needs; and business and professional organizations. Expeditionary Learning Schools Outward Bound offers a whole school reform model to more than 150 elementary and secondary schools throughout the country. Similarly, the National Outdoor Leadership School (NOLS) takes people of all ages on remote wilderness expeditions, teaching technical outdoor skills, leadership, and environmental ethics in some of the world's wildest and most awe-inspiring classrooms. What NOLS teaches cannot be learned in a classroom or on a city street. It takes practice to learn outdoor skills and time to develop leadership. The wilderness provides the ideal setting for this unique education.

For more information, visit www.outwardbound.org or www.nols.edu.

2. Try Public Achievement

Public Achievement is a youth civic engagement initiative focused on the most basic concepts of citizenship, democracy, and public work. Public Achievement draws on the talents and desires of ordinary people to build a better world and to create a different kind of politics. Its work is anchored by these core ideas:

1. *Everybody can do citizen work.* All people—regardless of age, nationality, sex, religion, income, or education—can be powerful public actors.

2. *Citizenship isn't easy.* Democracy is messy and sometimes frustrating, but when you work hard with others you can accomplish extraordinary things.

3. *We learn by doing.* The most important lessons of democracy come from doing public work and finding ways to cooperate with people who are different and may disagree.

To learn more, visit www.augsburg.edu/cdc/publicachievement.

3. Create Something "Instructable"

Instructables is a web-based documentation platform where passionate people share what they do and how they do it, and learn from and collaborate with others. The seeds of Instructables germinated at the MIT Media Lab, as the future founders of Squid Labs built places to share their projects and help others. To create a new Instructable, comment on someone else's Instructable, or do lots of other cool things, visit www.instructables.com.

4. Explore Project-Based Learning

In project-based learning (PBL), students go through an extended process of inquiry in response to a complex question, problem, or challenge. While allowing for some degree of student "voice and choice," rigorous projects are carefully planned, managed, and assessed to help students learn key academic content; practice twenty-first-century skills such as collaboration, communication, and critical thinking; and create high-quality, authentic products and presentations.

To learn more about PBL, visit the Buck Institute for Education at www.bie.org.

5. Share Your Story

StoryCorps is an independent nonprofit whose mission is to provide Americans of all backgrounds and beliefs with the opportunity to record, share, and preserve the stories of our lives. Each conversation is recorded on a free CD to share and is preserved at the American Folklife Center at the Library of Congress. StoryCorps is one of the largest oral history projects of its kind: millions of people listen to its weekly broadcasts on NPR's *Morning Edition* and on its own Listen pages. To learn how to record your personal story, visit storycorps.org.

EPILOGUE

In Memoriam

George Wood

When I think of powerful learning stories, I think of Ted Sizer. Not that he told such stories himself (although he did that too, through his books), but how well he *listened* to the stories of others.

In his books, Ted told us what powerful learning experiences could be for all of our children. He could tell those stories because he had spent a lifetime collecting them. Everyone who knew Ted can remember his thoughtful questions, and how—hand on head, pencil at the ready—he would listen and note carefully the response. "What do you mean by ...?" "Tell me more about ..." "Can you imagine it another way?" Carefully, respectfully, and earnestly, Ted plumbed the depths of any learning story in order to learn about learning and what people need in order for it to happen.

As a result of his careful listening, Ted drew the primary lessons that would be reflected in his teaching. As a professor, dean, head of school, teacher of teachers, and leader of one of the most vibrant school support organizations the nation has seen, he taught us all what it means to help young people use their minds well.

That's what the stories in this book are about as well. If you listened carefully as you read them, you too have found a shared vision of what powerful learning actually *looks like*—a vision that we at the Forum for Education and Democracy believe should be guiding all we do to make our public schools the sorts of learning communities our democracy needs.

These fifty stories remind us that we need more schools where learning unfolds in a supportive environment, with students and teachers working side by side on developing new understandings and competencies. We need schools where all students are challenged with high standards that apply to everyone—and not just a select few. We need places where learning is experiential and students are out learning in the community as well as the classroom. We need schools that make the learning process relevant and connected to the lives and concerns of young people. And we need communities of engagement where the content of the learning is designed to speak to who students are and what they can become.

I can think of no better way to honor Ted's legacy than by acting upon some of what we have heard in this collection. Together we can advocate for schools that are challenging, engaging, supportive, relevant, and experiential. And we can do this on behalf of not only every child, but also the future of our democracy—which requires a system of public schooling that enables us all to use our minds well in exercising our individual rights and civic responsibilities.

TED SIZER

1932–2009

My first real teaching was in the army, where, as a twenty-one-year-old lieutenant in the artillery, I needed to teach my charges—mostly Puerto Rican high school dropouts who were as old or older than I was—how to prepare howitzers to fire at objects that were miles away. It was an important and practical form of geometry, a subject at which I had not been very successful in school. By now I was good at it, but I feared that learning would be too difficult for them, and then we would all fail.

I learned then that most teachers need to learn before they can teach. They have to learn about their students—and especially about what is relevant to them. My students were determined not to hit the wrong target; they struggled with the guns' sights' calibrations until they got them right. They took care of the ammunition so that it wouldn't grow too wet or too dry. They followed all the safety precautions as if they had written the manual themselves. Where they came from, the learning difficulties they had had in the past, the many differences between their childhoods and mine, even what language they spoke mattered less than the job we had to do together. They did their new work successfully and gave me something I have valued ever since: faith in the possibilities for learning if teachers and students align their incentives.

SAM CHALTAIN

Hometown: Hanover, New Hampshire

Current home: Washington, D.C.

My ideal school is a place where: all children have the skills and self confidence they need to be seen and heard in meaningful, responsible ways

My personal heroes: Vic Chaltain, Charles Haynes, Roger Williams

My personal motto: Do your work, then step back: the only path to serenity

My idea of perfect happiness: a day with my family and nothing to do but decide how best to spend it

My present state of mind: on the path …

Quotable: "What would happen if, rather than thinking of democracy as something we inherit, like a suit of clothes passed on from our grandparents, we thought of it as a learning process—one where we've only taken the smallest baby steps so far."—C. Otto Scharmer

Please note: The author website has moved from rethinklearningnow.com to facesoflearning.net

■ - - - - - - - - - ■

Sam Chaltain is a Washington, D.C.–based writer, educator, and organizational change consultant. He works with schools and both public and private sector companies to help them create healthy, high functioning learning environments.

Sam's writings about his work have appeared in both magazines and newspapers, including *Education Week, USA Today,* and *The Huffington Post,* where he blogs regularly. A periodic contributor to CNN and MSNBC, Sam is also the author or coauthor of five books. To learn more, visit www.samchaltain.com.

ABOUT RETHINK LEARNING NOW

The Rethink Learning Now campaign is a national coalition of education and civil organizations that share a commitment to change the tenor of our national conversation about schooling—by shifting it from a culture of testing, in which we overvalue basic-skills reading and math scores and undervalue just about everything else, to a culture of learning, in which we restore our collective focus on the core conditions of a powerful learning environment and work backward from there to decide how best to evaluate and improve our schools, our educators, and the progress of our nation's schoolchildren.

A list of all participating organizations is provided below. To learn more, and to share your own personal story, visit www.facesoflearning.net.

ADVANCEMENT PROJECT

The Advancement Project, a policy, communications, and legal action group committed to racial justice, was founded by a team of veteran civil rights lawyers in 1998. Their mission is to develop, encourage, and widely disseminate innovative ideas and pioneer models that inspire and mobilize a broad national racial justice movement to achieve universal opportunity and a just democracy.

www.advancementproject.org

ALL KINDS OF MINDS

All Kinds of Minds helps educators and schools broaden their understanding and appreciation of how students learn and vary in their learning. Their research-based training and tools enable teachers to leverage new research on learning in their work with students, particularly those who struggle with learning. They believe that all students should have the opportunity to find success in learning, all teachers should be learning experts, and all schools should be able to serve the needs of their diverse learners equitably. They believe that once teachers understand how students learn and put that understanding into practice—every day, with every student—achievement gaps will close, disengaged students will decrease in number, and the chronic underperformance of students in our schools will diminish.

www.allkindsofminds.org

ALLIANCE FOR CHILDHOOD

The Alliance for Childhood is a partnership of individuals and organizations committed to providing a healthier, more creative childhood for all children. It focuses on areas critical to children's well-being, including the restoration of play.

www.allianceforchildhood.org

AMERICAN ASSOCIATION OF COLLEGES FOR TEACHER EDUCATION

The American Association of Colleges for Teacher Education (AACTE) is a national alliance of educator preparation programs dedicated to the highest-quality professional development of teachers and school leaders in order to enhance PK–12 student learning.

www.aacte.org

ANTIOCH CENTER FOR SCHOOL RENEWAL

The Antioch Center for School Renewal has twenty-five years of experience providing high-quality professional development for educators across New England. As the service division of the Department of Education at Antioch University New England, their unique staff of highly skilled, experienced K–12 teacher-leaders and core university faculty are part of an educational institution that dates back to Horace Mann and embodies the values of progressive, student-centered education.

The mission of the Antioch Center for School Renewal is to support and nurture the creation of equitable, inspiring, personalized learning communities and to make them the common experience for young people and educators everywhere.

www.antiochne.edu/acsr

ASPIRA

ASPIRA is the only national Hispanic organization dedicated exclusively to developing the educational and leadership capacity of Hispanic youth. Since 1961, ASPIRA has been working at the grassroots level to provide programs that encourage

Hispanic students to stay in school and prepare them to succeed in the educational arena, develop their leadership skills, and serve their community.

www.aspira.org

CENTER FOR CIVIC EDUCATION

The Center for Civic Education is a nonprofit, nonpartisan educational corporation dedicated to promoting an enlightened and responsible citizenry committed to democratic principles and actively engaged in the practice of democracy in the United States and other countries. The center specializes in civic and citizenship education, law-related education, and international educational exchange programs for developing democracies. Programs focus on the U.S. Constitution and Bill of Rights; American political traditions and institutions at the federal, state, and local levels; constitutionalism; civic participation; and the rights and responsibilities of citizens.

www.civiced.org

CENTER FOR COLLABORATIVE EDUCATION

The mission of the Center for Collaborative Education (CCE) is to transform schools to ensure that all students succeed. They believe that schools should prepare every student to achieve academically and make a positive contribution to a democratic society. CCE partners with public schools and districts to create and sustain effective and equitable schools.

www.ccebos.org

CENTER FOR INSPIRED TEACHING

Center for Inspired Teaching is an educational reform organization in Washington, D.C., dedicated to ensuring schools make the most of children's innate desire to learn. They do this by investing in teachers through courses and mentoring, school partnerships, research, and advocacy. The center's programs embrace both accountability and creativity as a means for raising student achievement. Since 1995, Center for Inspired Teaching has provided training for more than 5,000 educators throughout the D.C. metropolitan area, improving instruction for over 125,000 students by creating the capacity for teachers to serve as agents of change in their classrooms, schools, and beyond.

www.inspiredteaching.org

COALITION OF ESSENTIAL SCHOOLS

The Coalition of Essential Schools (CES) is at the forefront of creating and sustaining personalized, equitable, and intellectually challenging schools. Essential schools are places of powerful learning where all students have the chance to reach their fullest potential. By coaching to create cultures of continuous improvement and powerful professional learning communities focused on student achievement, CES works with educators to support and promote innovative and effective teaching. CES works with school districts and other entities to shape the policy conditions that support and promote schools characterized by personalization, democracy and equity, intellectual vitality and excellence, and graduates who experience success in all aspects of their lives: educational, professional, civic, and personal.

www.essentialschools.org

EDUCATION LAW CENTER

Founded in 1973, Education Law Center (ELC) advocates on behalf of public school children for access to an equal and adequate education under state and federal laws. ELC's work is based on a core value: if given the opportunity, all children can achieve high academic standards to prepare them for citizenship and to thrive in the economy.

www.edlawcenter.org

EDVISIONS

EdVisions' mission is to create schools that will enhance relationships and build relevant learning environments that empower students, parents, and teachers to make choices. These learning environments utilize self-directed, project-based learning to build student autonomy through relevant learning opportunities;

create student belongingness through full-time advisories; and empower teachers via teacher-managed, democratically collaborative schools. EdVisions has two divisions: one focuses on school development, including ongoing school coaching; and the other, EdVisions Leader Center, supports school development through best-practice dissemination, institutes, research, and a variety of technical assessment tools.

www.edvisions.com

FAIRTEST

The National Center for Fair and Open Testing (FairTest) advances quality education and equal opportunity by promoting fair, open, valid, and educationally beneficial evaluations of students, teachers, and schools. FairTest also works to end the misuses and flaws of testing practices that impede those goals.

FairTest.org

THE FIVE FREEDOMS PROJECT

The Five Freedoms Project is a national organization that provides leadership development, coaching, and support to address two of America's greatest challenges at the same time: improving the performance of our public schools and strengthening the quality of our civic discourse.

www.fivefreedoms.org

THE FORUM FOR EDUCATION AND DEMOCRACY

The Forum for Education and Democracy is a national education "action tank" committed to the public, democratic role of public education—the preparation of engaged and thoughtful democratic citizens. The forum works to promote a public education system worthy of a democracy, one characterized by strong public schools, equity of educational resources, and an informed, involved citizenry.

ForumForEducation.org

FOXFIRE

Foxfire is a nonprofit educational and literary organization based in Rabun County, Georgia. Founded in 1966, Foxfire's learner-centered, community-based educational approach is advocated through both a regional demonstration site grounded in the southern Appalachian culture that gave rise to Foxfire (the Foxfire Museum and Heritage Center), and a national program of teacher training and support that promotes a sense of place and appreciation of local people, community, and culture as essential educational tools (the Foxfire Approach to Teaching and Learning).

Foxfire.org

IDEA

What if all young people had the freedom to be creative, curious, collaborative learners? IDEA envisions an American education system based on respect for human rights and democratic values of freedom and responsibility, participation and collaboration, and equity and justice. IDEA seeks to frame the national dialogue about education, build a diverse network of participants, and catalyze sustainable action at the local, regional, and national levels.

www.democraticeducation.org

JUSTICE MATTERS

Justice Matters is a national racial justice movement building organization focusing on creating education policy rooted in community vision. Justice Matters employs a comprehensive multitiered approach that includes community organizing, communications, and policy. They believe that young people of color thrive in public schooling that engages each student's brilliance and communities through joyful, culturally responsible practices. This educational experience prepares the next generation of leaders to build a more just and healthy world.

www.justicematters.org

KNOWLEDGE NOTEBOOK

Knowledge NoteBook is a Virginia-based company dedicated to the promotion of learning via its free software product. The software in essence simplifies learning.

www.knowledgenotebook.com

NAACP

The mission of the National Association for the Advancement of Colored People is to ensure the political, educational, social, and economic equality of rights of all persons and eliminate racial hatred and racial discrimination.

www.naacp.org

NATIONAL ALLIANCE OF BLACK SCHOOL EDUCATORS

The National Alliance of Black School Educators (NABSE) is dedicated to improving both the educational experiences and accomplishments of African American youth through the development and use of instructional and motivational methods that increase levels of inspiration, attendance, and overall achievement.

www.nabse.org

NATIONAL CONGRESS OF AMERICAN INDIANS

The NCAI was founded in 1944 in response to termination and assimilation policies that the United States federal government forced on the tribal governments in contradiction of their treaty rights and status as sovereigns. NCAI works to secure the rights and benefits to which American Indians are entitled, to enlighten the public toward a better understanding of the Indian people, to preserve rights under Indian treaties or agreements with the United States, and to promote the common welfare of the American Indians and Alaska Natives.

www.ncai.org

NATIONAL NETWORK FOR EDUCATIONAL RENEWAL

The National Network for Educational Renewal (NNER) leads by example as it strives to improve simultaneously the quality of education for thoughtful participation in a democracy and the quality of the preparation of educators. The NNER's twenty-four settings throughout the United States and Canada comprise partnerships among P–12 schools, institutions of higher education, and communities.

www.nnerpartnerships.org

NEW YORK PERFORMANCE STANDARDS CONSORTIUM

The New York Performance Standards Consortium, a coalition of thirty-one small, diverse public high schools across New York state, exemplifies education reform based on a strong commitment to school-as-community; ongoing professional development; and active, inquiry-based learning. Consortium schools have designed a system of challenging performance-based assessments to gauge student learning and fulfill graduation requirements.

www.performanceassessment.org

NATURAL LEARNING RESEARCH INSTITUTE

The Natural Learning Research Institute is a nonprofit organization dedicated to researching and introducing natural learning into education at all levels. It was created by individuals from many educational settings, including public and private schools, university professors and researchers, the public service, and human resource development. The institute's work is grounded in the system principles of natural learning developed by Renate and Geoffrey Caine and on the theory and processes that they have been developing and testing for almost twenty years. It constantly explores other fields of research that support its efforts, including current understanding about the nature of expertise, the design and impact of video games, authentic leadership, organizational development, communities of practice, and systems theory.

www.naturallearninginstitute.org

THE NEW DEEL

The mission of the New DEEL is to create an action-oriented partnership dedicated to inquiry into the nature and practice of democratic, ethical educational leadership through sustained processes of open dialogue, right to voice, community inclusion, and responsible participation toward the common good. They strive to create an environment to facilitate democratic, ethical decision making in educational theory and practice that acts in the best interest of all students.

newdeel.ning.com

THE ORION SOCIETY

Since 1982, Orion has published work that challenges conventional wisdom and offers ideas to promote cultural and environmental change. Since that time, programs in education and grassroots activism have been added, as have workshops and conferences. Orion has pioneered an approach called Place-Based Education and offers a summer workshop called Educating in a Changing Climate. Its current education focus is promoting whole-child alternatives to narrow accountability mandates. The evolving mission of the Orion Society—which together with the Myrin Institute publishes *Orion* magazine—is to inform, inspire, and engage individuals and grassroots organizations in becoming significant cultural forces for healing nature and community.

www.orionsociety.org

PLUSTIME NH

PlusTime NH strives for a day when every child in New Hampshire is safe, supported, and inspired after school. The mission of PlusTime NH is to provide the guidance, leadership, and support essential to improve and sustain after-school programs in New Hampshire communities. They do this by providing funding, professional development, and human resources to the after-school field in New Hampshire.

www.plustime.org

PUBLIC EDUCATION NETWORK

Public Education Network (PEN) is a national constituency of local education funds and individuals working to increase student achievement and advance public school reform in low-income communities across America. PEN believes that an active, vocal constituency is key to ensuring that every child, in every community, benefits from a quality public education.

www.publiceducation.org

PUBLIC SCHOOLS FOR TOMORROW

Public Schools for Tomorrow is a national group of public school superintendents, former superintendents, and friends. Their goal is to bring about fundamental change in the schools and in society so that all children learn to high standards, nurture their personal growth and talents, and develop their capacities.

www.publicschoolsfortomorrow.org

RETHINKING SCHOOLS

Rethinking Schools began in 1986 as a local effort to create classrooms for hope and social justice, as an alternative to test-driven standardization. It has grown into a prominent publisher of educational materials and a national voice for grassroots educators committed to social justice. Rethinking Schools is an activist project, addressing both classroom and policy issues with materials written by and for teachers, parents, and students.

www.rethinkingschools.org

SMALL SCHOOLS WORKSHOP

The Small Schools Workshop is a group of educators, organizers, and researchers who work in collaboration with teachers, principals, parents, and district leaders to create new, small, innovative learning communities in public schools.

www.smallschools.com

SPARK

Spark is the only youth empowerment program in the country that addresses the dropout crisis by reengaging at-risk students through one-on-one apprenticeships. These workplace-based apprenticeships—in professions each student has identified as a "dream job"—are complemented by a leadership curriculum, workshops, and field trips. The Spark experience creates a powerful sense of relevance for students, while providing the skills and confidence needed to be successful in school and in life.

www.sparkprogram.org

STRENGTHS MOVEMENT

The Strengths Movement is a nonprofit organization that helps young people discover their unique paths in life by leveraging their strengths, rather than focusing on their weaknesses. They believe that young people who discover their activity, relationship, and learning strengths will experience greater success, satisfaction, and significance by understanding how to make a meaningful contribution in life. They do this by working with parents, teachers, schools, and organizations responsible for the care and raising of young people. Their goal is to put technology-based, media-driven strengths development tools into the hands of two million teens by 2015.

www.strengthsmovement.com

THE TEACHER SALARY PROJECT

The Teacher Salary Project addresses the urgent need for a complete cultural shift in the way our society values effective teachers. Based on the *New York Times* bestselling book *Teachers Have It Easy*, the project's feature-length documentary film, social media, and advocacy outreach campaign tell the collective story of the 3.2 million teachers in America and their critical role in our democracy.

www.theteachersalaryproject.org

UNITED CHURCH OF CHRIST JUSTICE AND WITNESS MINISTRIES

The United Church of Christ Justice and Witness Ministries' mission is to speak and act prophetically through community mobilization, leadership training, issues education, public witness, and public policy advocacy in support of the social action policies of the United Church of Christ's General Synod, its biennial governing body. Historically the United Church of Christ has worked to strengthen public schools, particularly for their public role in our democracy, and has spoken out against policies that weaken public education—including inequity, racism and xenophobia, an excessive focus on standardization and high-stakes testing, and privatization.

www.ucc.org/justice/public-education

UNIVERSITY COUNCIL FOR EDUCATIONAL ADMINISTRATION

The University Council for Educational Administration (UCEA) is an international consortium of prestigious research universities committed to advancing the preparation and practice of educational leaders for the benefit of children, schools, and society. As a consortium, UCEA symbolizes an important aspiration: advancing significantly the field of educational leadership through interinstitutional cooperation, communication, and contribution.

www.ucea.org

WORLDBLU

The purpose of WorldBlu is to unleash human potential and inspire freedom by championing the growth of organizational democracy worldwide. Their vision is to build a more democratic world, one organization at a time, and their goal is to encourage the creation of twenty thousand democratic workplaces around the world by 2020. They inspire and support this global movement by offering a range of programs and services that enable business leaders to design, develop, and lead the most successful democratic organizations in the world.

www.worldblu.com

ACKNOWLEDGMENTS

Faces of Learning is the result of a grassroots campaign in which nearly forty education and civil rights organizations joined forces to urge the country to Rethink Learning Now.

For making it all possible, I wish to thank my former colleagues at the Forum for Education and Democracy, who helped launch the campaign and who continue to provide some of the most important thought leadership in the country around issues of K–12 school improvement.

The Ford Foundation's Fred Frelow and Jeannie Oakes were responsible for providing the campaign with financial support—a reflection of their belief in the power of collaboration and of individual voices contributing to a shared vision of what children need to learn to use their minds well.

When the manuscript was in its final stages, Andrea Cahn, Michael Soguero, Dan Condon, Kim Carter, Jenerra Williams, Cyn Savo, Renee Moore, Tatyana Varshavsky, Aleta Margolis, and Clare Struck helped shape the resources that appear at the back of each chapter—either reminding me of things I'd forgotten or introducing me to new ideas and programs that will now, thanks to them, have the chance to reach a wider audience.

There are several people whose time and effort have been most essential to the overall success of the campaign and, by extension, the book: Maya Rockeymoore, Susan Oliver, Bill McIntyre, Kevin McCann, Mark Maloney, Paul Kittredge, Abbey Kos, Jim Freeman, Alexi Nunn, Heather Harding and Laura Bornfreund. Of all of us, Laura was the primary engine—connecting our different organizations, keeping us on schedule, and sharing her ideas about how our work could be more effective. This book is a tribute to her outstanding work.

Finally, *Faces of Learning* is what it is thanks to the many hundreds of people across the country who stopped what they were doing long enough to share a deeply personal and meaningful story from their past. Our shared memories of learning and teaching, if we choose to heed them, can illuminate a path to school renewal in every community. In that spirit, I hope everyone reading this book will take the time to not just reflect on and share their own story, but also serve as a catalyst in their community and urge everyone they know to do the same.

Together we can change the tenor of the national conversation about schooling—one story at a time.

PHOTO CREDITS

Jenna Fournel, photo courtesy of Elizabeth Sander.

Mark Rockeymoore, photo courtesy of Maya Rockeymoore.

Jan Resseger, photo courtesy of United Church of Christ Publishing, Identity, and Communication Ministry.

Gloria Ladson-Billings, photo courtesy of Ming Fong.

Loretta Goodwin, photo courtesy of David Goodwin.

Bruce Deitrick Price, photo courtesy of Contemporary Art Center.

Arne Duncan, photo courtesy of United States Department of Education.

Angela Valenzuela, photo courtesy of Marsha Miller.

Carl Glickman, photo courtesy of Noah Stapper.

Andrew Margon, photo courtesy of the author.

Renee Moore, photo courtesy of Milken Family Foundation.

Amy Estersohn, photo courtesy of Emilia Mickevicius.

Maritza Brito, photo courtesy of Wendy L. Clinton.

Kevin McCann, photo courtesy of Alex McCann.

Margaret Owens, photo courtesy of Kay Tousley.

Larry Myatt, photo courtesy of Facing History, Facing Ourselves.

John Goodlad, photo courtesy of Paula McMannon.

Sitembiso Ncube Maduma, photo courtesy of Carol Ncube.

Elijah Cummings, photo courtesy of United States House of Representatives.

Jill Vialet, photo courtesy of Elizabeth Cushing.

Al Franken, photo courtesy of United States Senate.

Jenifer Fox, photo courtesy of Chris Macke.

Michelle Durange, photo courtesy of the author.

Zainab Ali, photo courtesy of Ben Gibbs.

Susan Oliver, photo courtesy of Sherri L. Ash Photography.

Gary Cohen, photo courtesy of the author.

Chantale Soekhoe, photo courtesy of Ranju Majumdar.

Emily Gasoi, photo courtesy of Ian Cook.

Cass Carland, photo courtesy of the author.

Carrie A. Rogers, photo courtesy of Jacob W. Deem.

R. Dwayne Betts, photo courtesy of Rachel Eliza Griffith.

Robert McLaughlin, photo courtesy of Carley Stevens-McLaughlin.

Deborah Meier, photo courtesy of Dody Riggs.

Jamal Fields, photo courtesy of Leslie Jue Fields.

Jenerra Williams, photo courtesy of the author.

Patrick Ip, photo courtesy of Jeff Srole.

Gerlma A. Johnson, photo courtesy of Dave Buoy.

Ahniwake Rose, photo courtesy of Wauhilleau Webb.

James Comer, photo courtesy of Yale University.

Joel Elliott, photo courtesy of Amina Ahmad.

Terry Pickeral (with his grandchildren Kenji and Logan), photo courtesy of Jennifer Pickeral.

Elizabeth Rogers, photo courtesy of H. Maurene Cooper.

Steve Moore, photo courtesy of Matt Almaraz.

Jill Davidson (with her children Leo, Henry, and Elias), photo courtesy of Kevin Eberman.

Rachel Barnes, photo courtesy of Cindy Macomber.

Stedman Graham, photo courtesy of Simon & Schuster.

Stephen Vick, photo courtesy of SMV Photography.

Liz Lerman, photo courtesy of Lise Metzger.

Maya Soetoro-Ng (with her daughter Suhaila), photo courtesy of Suhaila Soetoro-Ng.

Ted Sizer (with his wife, Nancy), photo courtesy of Roger Warner.